Ghosts of Su

Ghosts
of
Sussex

Judy Middleton

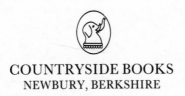

COUNTRYSIDE BOOKS
NEWBURY, BERKSHIRE

First Published 1988
© Judy Middleton 1988
Reprinted 1990

ISBN 0 905392 90 6

Produced through MRM Associates Ltd., Reading
Typeset by Acorn Bookwork, Salisbury, Wiltshire
Printed in England by J.W. Arrowsmith, Bristol

Ghosts! There are nigh a thousand million walking the earth openly at noontide; some half-hundred have vanished from it, some half-hundred have arisen in it, ere thy watch ticks once.

Carlyle

Contents

The
Junk Shop Ghost

A JUNK shop occupied the ground floor of a house near the junction of Upper Rock Gardens and Edward Street, Brighton in the 1950s. When Mr. R. McColl, a second hand book dealer called at the shop the proprietor was busy and suggested that he came back to look at the books after the shop was closed. McColl was quite happy to do this because he would be able to take his time in looking through them so he took the keys and agreed to hand them over to the woman living upstairs when he had finished.

It was about 8 o'clock in the evening when McColl made his way down into the gloomy old kitchen where the books were stored. He took two candles with him because he had been warned that there was no lighting down there. The most striking feature of the room was a huge stone sink of the size of a horse trough. The sink was set into an alcove which had an arch decorated with a zig-zag pattern of thin red bricks. He lit the candles and placed one on a sideboard near the archway and the other on the table where he was going to examine the books.

As he flicked through the pages of the various volumes he began to feel a sense of unease. At the same time he felt an icy chill and he became aware that his hair was bristling. He thought perhaps he was sickening for flu but he decided to persist in his examination. All the same he could not get rid of the notion that somebody was watching him. Looking up he saw that a cloud had formed in the archway. He walked towards it to reassure himself that nothing was there.

He returned to the books once more and he had just found a book he wanted particularly and had placed it to one side when he looked up again and saw that the cloud had resolved itself into the shape of a woman. It gave him a dreadful fright not because the spectre was a naked woman but because it resembled a repulsive corpse with swollen and distorted limbs. He managed to ask the apparition hoarsely what she wanted but he did not expect a reply, it was merely an immediate reaction on his part. His next action was inspired by fright; he picked up a book and flung it at the ghost. It passed straight through her and hit the wall beyond.

By this time Mr McColl had had enough so he gathered up his belongings and went upstairs to hand over the keys. The woman who lived upstairs was greatly surprised that he had been allowed down there alone and in the dark. She said she would not go down there at any price. It transpired that she had once seen the ghost on the stairs and it had passed straight through her body leaving her chilled to the bone and subject to bouts of shivering for weeks afterwards. Furthermore after she had run back to her flat and locked the door, she said the thing kept flopping against it for a whole hour afterwards.

No wonder the poor woman did not want a repeat experience. By this time McColl had lost his fright and he began to be interested in the ghost and to wonder what facts lay behind the haunting. He discovered that some 60 years before (and he was telling the story in the 1950s) a man had murdered his wife and dumped the body in the sink where he proceeded to dismember it. His aim was to bury the bits under the stone floor of the kitchen and so leave no evidence of his crime. But the story goes that he was discovered before he had time to finish the deed.

Haunted Inns

WHEN Mr. Bill Harman and his wife Elsie moved into the *Stag Inn* in Kemp Town, Brighton in 1979 nobody said anything to them about a ghost. The pub predates the Kemp Town development and is over 300 years old. It used to be a coaching inn.

The first person to see the ghost was the Harman's son-in-law Joe Prothoe who had helped the Harmans with the move and was spending the night sleeping in the kitchen. In the early hours Joe came running upstairs with his hair standing on end because he had just seen a ghost. He said the figure was of a tall man wearing a large apron and he had a black band around each arm. The ghost walked straight through a wall. Since then Mr. Harman has seen the same figure himself in the corridor. He and the pub regulars, who were naturally very interested in the goings-on, decided to call the ghost Albert. Their theory was that he was a former landlord.

Albert made his presence felt in other ways too. One of his favourite tricks being to disconnect the keg beer gas lines, which has happened quite often. An idea which causes amusement to the regulars is that Albert might be expressing his disapproval of modern beverages and a barrel of beer has also been flung down the stairs when nobody was about. Certainly Albert never lays so much as a ghostly finger on the taps of the real ale!

The Harmans grew quite used to Albert. They respected his right to stay on at the *Stag* if he felt like it and after all he had done nothing spiteful. Therefore they had no intention of approaching anyone to come and exorcise the place. This acceptance probably caused Albert to quieten down because by September 1983 Mr. Harman said that Albert had not done anything for over a year. One had the impression that he was quite sorry about it!

Though the pub has since changed hands, Albert has not disappeared and is still around playing his favourite trick of turning off the keg beer!

Overlooking Sidlesham Quay stands the historic inn called the *Crab and Lobster* which until the 18th century was known as the *Swallow* inn. Presumably the ghost who haunted the premises would remember it as the *Swallow*. His presence was felt most strongly up in the attic and Mr. Brian Fairey, barman, said in 1974 that he would not venture up there, day or night. Many people have seen the ghost and describe him as a tall man dressed in uniform and wearing a cloak and riding boots.

The popular legend behind the haunting is that during the Civil War after Chichester had fallen to the Roundheads, the Royalist Sir Robert Earnley, his two nephews and some friends rode to Sidlesham hoping to embark for France. But they were pursued by a troop of Parliamentary soldiers and a fierce fight ensued on the quayside. The nephews were killed and Sir Robert was carried into the inn mortally wounded. Another version of the story is that all the Cavaliers except one were killed, either by the sword or by drowning as they tried to escape across the mudflats. The survivor fled to the *Swallow*. Unfortunately the Roundheads decided to celebrate their success at the inn and the Cavalier was discovered. He was killed at once.

The ghost was exorcised some years ago. But if the ghost is now quiet, the legend lives on and people are still turning up asking about him, some from as far afield as Canada!

Pubs are supposed to be places of good cheer and especially so when the landlord is a popular man. George Gutsell, landlord of the *Queen's Head* at Icklesham, was so well liked that when he died at about the turn of the century, his customers and friends decided to give him a rousing send-off. His coffin was brought into the pub and everyone drank his health. George himself must have appreciated the gesture heartily, so much so that he was reluctant to leave his pub. His ghost was often seen sitting in his favourite chair dressed in waistcoat and shirt sleeves — an old man with a beard. But there was nothing in the least ethereal about him; he looked as solid as the next man. Mr. Tony Crumdell was landlord of the *Queen's Head* for 25 years and saw George quite often, as did many other people. Even today, George's comfortable chair is kept ready for him and even sometimes a glass of whiskey placed ready beside it to encourage him, but his visits are now rare.

The Castle at Chichester boasts no common or garden ghost but a Roman centurion no less! People have inferred that the ghost was a centurion by the imperious way he causes the doors to open when he stalks through the place. The Castle is built hard by a section of the old Roman wall. The first Roman defences at Chichester were built at the end of the 2nd century AD and a century later they were rebuilt and strengthened. They were built to enclose an area of 90 acres in which some 2,000 people lived. It was a time of unrest and declining Roman power in Britain. The nearby Palace at Fishbourne was destroyed by fire at the end of the 3rd century AD so one can imagine how anxiously a centurion would pace the walls of Chichester.

The *Red Lion* at Hooe was built in 1595 overlooking the tidal marshland (as it then was) and it has been an inn since the early 17th century. Many pubs lay claim to being original smugglers' inns but the *Red Lion*'s claim is entirely valid. It has the ghost of a smuggler to prove it! An old tobacco mill still rests in the attic. It was locally made of wood and iron and the machine was used to shred the tobacco which arrived in smuggled bales of tobacco leaves. It is said that although the machine is still now, the noise of the illegal grinding can be heard to this day.

The present landlord is Mr. Keith Barton who took over from his father in 1968. The *Red Lion* has been in the hands of the same family for three generations. During all those years the Barton family and their resident ghost have grown used to each other.

Mr. Barton's father tells the story of how he woke up early one morning and saw the ghost standing at the foot of the bed. He was wearing an old fashioned long overcoat with full shoulders and he walked towards the wall where he vanished. The wall the ghost was heading for is in fact a built-in cupboard and, by flicking a peg part of the panelling, it opens inwards and provides direct access to the attic in the roof. It is difficult not to see this ghost as belonging to an old smuggler, retracing his footsteps to the illegal tobacco mill in the attic.

Early one evening a customer was sitting at the bar quietly sipping his beer when suddenly he hurried over to the other side of the room. On being asked the reason he explained that he had seen a man dressed in a long old fashioned greatcoat come out of one of the doors and head across the room towards the Ladies. The customer, being helpful, rushed over and said 'Sorry mate, you can't go in there' but the man vanished. The customer was a little shaken because the ghost had looked so solid and ordinary except for his old fashioned coat.

The King's Head at Cuckfield has a ghost with a colourful name. She has been dubbed Geranium Jane by the pub's employees (with a touch of black humour!) because geraniums are supposed to have been the cause of her untimely death. The story goes that a young girl who was a servant at the *King's Head* was seduced by her employer. When she became pregnant her lover either became worried or disenchanted. At any rate he dropped a pot of geraniums on top of poor Jane's head as she was passing beneath the window. Since then her ghost has haunted the pub and, not surprisingly, she prefers to disturb men. If any man connected with the pub is having an affair Geranium Jane gets particularly upset and she will come and give the bed a good shake in the middle of the night, while at the same time causing the temperature to plummet!

Some children have seen Geranium Jane. Two of them were playing quite happily upstairs while their mother was working in the bar when at midday they rushed downstairs saying they had seen a woman with make-up on her face. What had frightened them was that the 'make-up' appeared to be streaming down her face. And a few years ago a cleaner was busy one morning downstairs and her little boy was playing with his toy cars in front of the fireplace when he startled his mother by asking her what those white hands were doing fluttering about. Since then Geranium Jane seems to have settled down.

The *King's Arms*, Rotherfield was certainly haunted in the early 1950s. A ghost was never seen but footsteps were heard and oddly enough it was always on an evening in June. At the time of the manifestations the landlord was the Sussex and England cricketer Maurice Tate. One June evening in 1953 Mrs. Kay Tate was in the bar with her son, daughter and daughter-in-law when suddenly they heard heavy footsteps running hurriedly up the stairs and along the passage. They thought there were intruders in the house so upstairs they all went to check. But there was nobody in the corridor or in any of the bedrooms which opened off it. These footsteps had been noticed first of all in 1952.

In June 1954 the new licensee Mr. Hilary Ball heard the footsteps again at about the same time as usual. Although he described the footsteps as 'hurried' he said the tread was light. On the next anniversary in June 1955 when everybody was confidently awaiting the footsteps, the ghost failed to walk.

One of the bedrooms was labelled by the Tate family as 'the special room'. Maurice Tate was once in this room when he felt somebody touch him. It was such a deliberate gesture that he thought it was one of his children and asking 'What do you want?' he turned round. But he was the only person in the room!

The Oak Inn at Ardingly was granted its first ale licence in 1725 so pints have been pushed across the bar for some considerable time. Three labourer's cottages were knocked into one to form the pub. It is an event which occurred when the cottages were three separate dwellings which causes the *Oak Inn* to be haunted. Legend has it that a man from one of the cottages abducted a young girl, who naturally feared the worst. She managed to escape and hid in the orchard at the back of the cottages. But it did not take long for the man to discover her hiding place and he was so incensed that he killed her on the spot. The poor girl has been walking the floor of the *Oak Inn* ever since.

People who have seen the ghost describe her as having long dark hair and she wears a grey cloak. The landlords are Mick and Dorothy Hart from London who although they have not seen the ghost themselves, have eye-witnesses amongst their regulars. One lady called Cheryll has seen her at about 6 p.m. and she appears from the back of the pub and walks towards the inglenook fireplace where she sits quietly.

One of the Hart's friends is a man who refuses to be left alone in the bar after having experienced a brush with the ghost. One night he was standing at the bar on his own when he felt a vigorous push on the back. Supposing that he had got in somebody else's way he turned round to apologise but there was nobody in the room.

What the Harts have noticed are odd incidents like a bunch of keys leaping off a table and the pint mugs suspended on hooks above the bar which started to swing by themselves. The Harts connect these events with the old settle being moved out of the inglenook in 1983. Apparently the ghost did not approve of this action at all. The settle was moved back.

But since then the settle has been moved again without obvious comment from the ghost. Perhaps she is resigned to it now.

Christine Pierce liked the atmosphere of the *Seven Stars* at Robertsbridge as soon as she stepped inside in the early 1980s. She also had a curious certainty that she and her husband would be offered the pub. However, it did not seem a likely prospect at the time because there were 69 other couples who also wanted the chance to run the historic pub, which dates back to the 14th century. But she was right and Mike and Christine Pierce and their three children moved into the *Seven Stars*. Christine did have her reservations though because she had been told the pub was haunted and she did not know how she would cope with that.

As with so many haunted houses, a change in tenancy seems to stir the resident ghost into activity. Chris had only been at the pub two nights when she heard the ghost walking about. It was at night and she was in bed. The footsteps sounded very loud stamping through the house. At the same time she felt totally immobilized and she lay there rigid with fright. She could not even speak to wake up her husband who was sleeping peacefully beside her.

The Pierce's cross-collie dog had a similar reaction at a certain place in the upstairs corridor. His fur stood up, his eyes bulged and he could not move. Chris had to pick him up and carry him downstairs. Once he was away from the cold spot he was perfectly normal again. Tradition says that the cold spot in the corridor marks the place where a Franciscan monk was hacked to death by some Roundheads during the Civil War and it is his ghost which haunts the *Seven Stars*. Some people call him the Red Monk after the colour of his habit. But the colour is russet brown rather than ruby red. The monk has white hair.

When the Pierces wanted to attend a friend's wedding they could not leave the pub unattended because of insurance conditions. An old friend called David said he would be happy to oblige. He is a down to earth fellow and an ex-naval officer so the Pierces had no qualms about leaving him on his own in a haunted pub. When the time came for David to go to bed he settled down quite comfortably. He had dropped off to sleep when suddenly he felt someone shaking him awake. Puzzled he got out of bed and checked the pub to make sure all was well. When he was certain there was nothing wrong he returned to bed and was soon fast asleep again. For the second time he was woken up by someone shaking him and pulling the bedcover away. So he got up and switched on the lights and toured the building as before. He tried to go to sleep afterwards but when he was disturbed a third and a fourth time he went downstairs muttering 'I give up' and spent the rest of the night awake. When the Pierces returned the first thing David said was 'Don't you ever ask me to spend a night here on my own again'. Later they discovered that three houses in Robertsbridge had been burgled that night and Chris likes to think a friendly spook was keeping an eye on the pub, and by keeping David awake had made sure the premises remained safe. A psychic friend told her that there was a sympathetic spirit present — presumably a different entity to that of the murdered monk.

Ghosts are one thing, but the *Seven Stars* also has poltergeist activity. Chris was washing up in the kitchen when about 15 mugs which were standing on the second shelf suddenly shot across the room and shattered against the wall. When there was a repeat performance with another person present Chris decided the shelf had better come down. So it was removed and this seemed to cure the problem. On another occasion Mike Pierce was busy upstairs when he heard voices talking in the cellar quite distinctly. He knew nobody was supposed to be there so he went down to investigate. He found nothing so he went back and resumed his work. When he heard the talking again he thought 'I'll catch the so and so's this time' and he raced down the stairs. As he did so he heard a terrific crash and when he arrived in the cellar he found an empty lager barrel had been flung across the room and was wedged in a corner while about 300 empty bottles had been tipped out of their crates and lay scattered all over the floor. But none of them was broken.

Not surprisingly the *Mermaid Inn* at Rye is one of the most photographed houses in Sussex. It has associations with the notorious Hawkhurst gang of smugglers and according to a witness they were once seen drinking at the inn, seated at the windows with their loaded pistols lying ready on the table. However, the ghost at the *Mermaid* does not seem to have any smuggling connections. Mrs. May Aldington bought the *Mermaid* just before the Second World War and she had heard about the supposed haunted chamber. So she and a female psychic decided to spend the night in it. They grew tired as they waited and they both fell asleep. Mrs. Aldington was woken up by the clash of steel and she was amazed to find a close-fought duel being enacted round her bed. The duellists were wearing doublet and hose and the fight was fast and furious until one of the combatants was killed. The victor then calmly hauled his victim to the corner of the room where he dumped him down an oubliette. The psychic woman slept through it all!

3

The Ghost
who loved Windmills

THE two windmills known as Jack and Jill stand on Duncton Down above the village of Clayton. They must be one of the most famous and best loved landmarks in Sussex. Jack, the black tower mill, has always stood there, having been built in 1866 to replace the old Duncton post-mill. But Jill, the white post-mill, started life as one of three windmills on the Dyke Road at Brighton and was moved to her present site in 1852. The mills ceased to work in 1907 since when they have been used as a holiday home or as a permanent residence.

A person who lives in an isolated mill needs a special sort of temperament with a touch of introspection — a writer for instance. And it is interesting to note that Henry Martin, and Captain Anson who lived there after Martin, and Henry Longhurst who came after Anson, were all writers.

In 1911 the Anson family came to live at the mills and they remained for over 40 years. They lived in a wooden bungalow converted from the old miller's and shepherd's cottages and they used Jack as workroom and storeroom. Conditions were primitive with no piped water or electricity. But perhaps it did not matter to the Ansons who came of tough seafaring stock. Mrs. Anson's father was Captain Cooper Coles and her husband was Captain Walter Anson. In a glass case mounted on the wall gleamed the medals struck for his famous forbear

Admiral Anson to commemorate his victory off Finisterre in 1747.

Captain Walter Anson produced biographies of Admirals Nelson, Warren and Jarvis while living at the mills. But it was his wife who was the moving force behind the place. It was she who created gardens and planted hedges and trees as windbreaks out of what had been bare Downland.

For forty years Mrs. Anson knew and loved the mills. She watched the seasons come and go and she came to know every creak and rustle the mills made in a high wind. She became so familiar with the wide vistas over the Weald that she could not imagine living anywhere else. When she died, of a chest infection, what could be more natural than that her ghost should remain in the place she loved so well.

In 1953 Jack and Jill were bought by Henry Longhurst, a witty man who numbered golfing and writing amongst his many interests. It became quite clear to the Longhursts that old Mrs. Anson, though dead, had not yet quitted the bungalow! Many times her characteristic cough could be heard coming from her old room — sometimes there was a guest sleeping there, sometimes the room was empty but it made no difference to the cough.

Perhaps Mrs. Anson was also responsible for ringing the bells. Captain Anson had instituted that classic upstairs/downstairs arrangement, a row of bells on the kitchen wall. The bells were connected to the various rooms and the wires even went along the underground passage and up into Jack and the old stump of Duncton. One day Mrs. Longhurst was talking to the builder in the kitchen when all six bells began ringing at once. It was not a case of hearing things either because both of them could see the bells moving. When the bells had stopped ringing, the builder opened a cupboard door and was startled to see an old broom zoom out at him, travelling fast and several inches off the ground.

On their very first night at the bungalow, Henry Longhurst

was woken up at 3.30 a.m. by a bell ringing, so to satisfy his curiosity he took his torch along to the kitchen and saw the third bell from the left swinging away. Another time Mrs. Longhurst and her mother were sitting over the fire in the Granary when a pair of tongs jumped across the fireplace.

It seems certain that the ghost of Mrs. Anson objected to strangers occupying her house but the hauntings did not bother the Longhursts in the slightest as they did not feel that the spirit of Mrs. Anson was malevolent. As time went by Mrs. Anson's ghost came to accept the situation. The manifestations became fewer as time passed and of course ended in 1963 when the old cottage cum bungalow was demolished and the Longhursts moved into a new house nearby with a low profile so as not to interfere with the skyline view of Jack and Jill.

4

Apparitions at Alfriston

ALFRISTON is one of the best known and frequently visited villages in Sussex and famous for its smuggling associations. It is only fitting that it should have some ghost stories too.

Dean's Place is near the Old Clergy House. At the end of the 19th century a woman was washing up in the back kitchen when she heard a gentle tap at the door. On saying 'Come in' there appeared a beautiful lady wearing a bright blue silk dress which rustled expensively as she stepped sedately through the room and then vanished. During alterations to the house at about the turn of the century a skeleton was found under a floor. If this skeleton had anything to do with the Lady in Blue it does not seem to have made any difference to her appearances. Dean's Place now serves as a hotel and the lady has been seen by several guests and she was seen by a 5 year old girl in the 1960s. Nobody seems to have any clue to her identity except to be sure she met a violent end. In its long history Dean's Place has had a number of different owners but no tradition exists linking the Lady in Blue to any particular one.

The White Way is the name given to that part of the Alfriston to Seaford road between Dean's Place and Frog Firle. The ghost of the young Chowne heir and/or his white dog used to walk the White Way every seven years it is said. But it was not a pleasant omen to see the ghost as it presaged bad luck. The story goes that in the 18th century the heir to the Chowne Estate at Place House, Frog Firle was out for an evening stroll with his faithful dog when he was ambushed by a gang of thieves. One of them was too heavy-handed with his club and young Chowne was killed. The terrified robbers hurriedly buried the body in a nearby field and were preparing to get out of the area fast when they heard the dog whining beside his master's makeshift grave. So they killed him too and buried him beside the road.

Seven years afterwards a young couple were walking along the White Way when they noticed a small white dog accompanying them who vanished into the bank. In the early 19th century the road was being widened and at the point where the dog had vanished, the workmen found the skeleton of a young man. The locals concluded it could only be the murdered young Chowne.

A house in Alfriston which had a Georgian core but a Victorian facade, had two ghosts, one inside and one outside. The latter was seen around the stable block (now demolished) and he was described as a white-haired old man with a long apron. The description fitted an old groom who had worked for the doctor who used to live in the house and visited his patients in his gig. Perhaps the groom had a real fondness for his horses but his continued presence around the stables long after he was dead certainly made flesh-and-blood horses nervous. A later family owned a pony who had a great dislike of the stable and had to be virtually pushed into it at night and once the stable door was closed the pony would kick at it. The ghost inside the house seems to have been a one-time governess. She was tall and grey-haired and she liked to tuck the young girl into her bed at night. The girl objected to this although of course she did not realize that her tucker-in was a ghost and not one of her mother's friends. The concerned parents stayed in her bedroom one night until the girl fell asleep and then they asked the ghost aloud to go away. The request seemed to have its effect because the little girl slept undisturbed from then on.

5

Theatrical Ladies in Grey

IT would be nice to know why the ghosts haunting two famous south coast theatres are both known as the Grey Lady. Both Grey Ladies are perfectly harmless ghosts although it can be quite a shock to see them unexpectedly.

The Grey Lady at the Theatre Royal, Brighton was seen in 1960 by the late Mr. Melville Gillam, the theatre's manager and she was seen again in 1970 by the late Mr. Jack Keates, the manager at that time. Mr. Keates saw her standing outside number one dressing room.

In 1981 the Grey Lady was seen by an usherette but the best documented sighting was in August 1982. At the time Alan Ayckbourn's comedy *Relatively Speaking* was playing at the theatre. Gerald Flood had a starring part and his wife Anne Flood was also with the company as its wardrobe mistress. Mrs. Flood was working backstage in the laundry room when she became conscious of a door banging away. She fully expected someone to go and shut it quickly but when nobody did she went to shut it herself. The banging door was at the end of a corridor which went past some of the dressing rooms. As she tried to shut the door securely she could feel a weight pushing from the other side. So instead of pushing the door shut, she pulled it open and there stood the Grey Lady. Anne Flood had such a clear close-up of the ghost that she said if she were an artist she would have been able to reproduce the face exactly. The ghost was between 50 and 60 years old and she wore a long grey dress with a tight waist and a full skirt. She had grey veiling on her head. Her face was very stern and some silvery hair hung in a fringe. Mrs. Flood stood rooted to the spot but the ghost merely swept past her after giving her a hard look. Strangely enough when Mr. Alan Harmsworth the storeman arrived for work that afternoon he remembered what a strange atmosphere there was in the theatre. It felt cold, clammy and musty. Less than an hour later he heard about Mrs. Flood and the Grey Lady.

The Grey Lady usually haunts the dressing room area but she has been seen in other parts of the theatre. In the early afternoon upstairs in the front part of the theatre, a woman who worked there once had the experience of a grey lady brushing past her in the corridor and vanishing into a blank wall. When one of the other staff members heard about it he was able to shed a little light on the matter because he was familiar with the history of the place. He said that the place where the ghost vanished was the bricked-up doorway to the old paybox. It dated back to the days when the customers did not all go in through one entrance to pay and the patrons of the cheaper seats paid upstairs.

One theory is that the Grey Lady is the ghost of Sarah Bernhardt famous for her portrayal of Marguerite Gauthier in *La Dame aux Camelias* once banned by the Lord Chamberlain because the heroine was a courtesan. When the ban was lifted the play became a great success and even Queen Victoria did not consider it too indelicate to sit through a performance!

However, there is no special reason why Sarah Bernhardt should haunt the Theatre Royal. She played Marguerite many times in many different theatres up and down the country.

Other strange occurrences at the Theatre Royal which might have something to do with the Grey Lady are as follows. In the 1970s Martin Jarvis was sitting in his dressing room removing his make-up after a first night performance when he felt a tap on his shoulder. He thought someone was saying 'Good Show' and congratulating him so he turned round smiling and there was nobody there.

Mr. Wayne King, the pianist who tours with the Danny La Rue show was on the opposite side of the building to the stage and dressing room area. He stepped out of the door onto the balcony and put his hand onto the balcony rail as he looked out over the street. But he had the odd sensation of his hand being frozen to the rail. He felt unable to move it.

Mr. Terry Caughell, electrician at the Connaught Theatre, Worthing, for 23 years has never seen the Grey Lady personally but the following stories have been told to him by eye-witnesses. Late one evening in the 1970s long after the performance was over, an actor was walking along the passage backstage. As he passed what was the old number one dressing room he happened to glance in the open door and he noted there was a lady in a long dress seated before the mirror applying make-up. It was not until he got to the end of the passage that he suddenly realized it was an odd time for an actress to be making-up when the show was over and everybody else had gone. So he retraced his footsteps but when he entered the number one dressing room it was empty.

The Connaught's Grey Lady is not particular about the time of day she appears. On another occasion in the 1970s the cleaners arrived at the theatre as usual at 7 a.m. to start work. One of them was soon busy in the former portrait gallery where exhibitions were held. There were mirrors on either side and the man could see what was happening behind him. As he worked he noticed a lady in a long grey dress go past him. He straightened up and said 'Good morning' but when he turned round there was nobody there. The story goes that the Grey Lady upset him so much that a glass of whisky had to be fetched to restore him to his normal self.

6

Phantoms of Herstmonceux Castle

A CASTLE built of red brick in the 1440s, complete with turrets and a moat should really have a ghost! Herstmonceux, for centuries the home of the Dacre family, lives up to its appearance with not one ghost but several.

One hundred years after the building of the castle there was a tragedy in the family. Sir Thomas Fiennes, Third Lord Dacre succeeded to the estate when he was barely 17 years old. Lord Dacre had youth, looks and wealth but he had the misfortune to have some boisterous friends who shared his liking for wine and his dislike for his near neighbour Sir Nicholas Pelham. On the eve of May Day in 1541 they had enjoyed a convivial evening together when one of them suggested out of the blue that it would be good sport to go and poach some deer from old Pelham's estate at Laughton. The idea met with popular support and off they rode in high spirits laughing and talking. In fact they made too much noise to be any success at poaching because their approach was heard by a group of Pelham's foresters who, mistrusting their motives, laid in wait to see what would happen. When the foresters plainly saw that it was the intention of the young men to kill some deer, they rushed out of their hiding place and a furious mêlée ensued. It was never clear exactly what happened because it was dark and there was a mass of men fighting each other and some say that Lord Dacre never took any part in the fighting at all. Be that as it may, one of the foresters John Bushbrig was mortally wounded and died two days later.

Lord Dacre and his seven friends were arrested and eventually tried. The unfortunate Lord Dacre was brought to the scaffold at Tyburn, and executed. Is it any wonder that the ghost of Lord Dacre should return to haunt Herstmonceux? He has been seen in the grounds, riding a fine, mettlesome horse and he wears large brass spurs and a rust-coloured cloak. When spoken to, both horse and rider plunge into the moat.

But it is a legend of a ghostly drummer which is synonymous with Herstmonceux. The apparition is reputedly not of a small boy but of a huge figure 9 feet tall who marches along the battlements with sparks flying from his drumsticks. Today it is generally assumed that such a story was put about by smugglers anxious to keep the locals away and the smugglers' contraband safe from prying eyes; the ruinous state of the castle in the 19th century certainly made an ideal hiding place. What is certain is that there was ghostly knocking heard at the castle and that the story was probably enlarged by the smugglers into a gigantic spectre. The cynics say that the ghostly drummer was laid not by exorcism but by the building of coastguard cottages on the coast!

There is a room in the castle called the Drummer's Hall. When Horace Walpole visited Herstmonceux in 1752 he was shown this room which he called 'a dismal chamber'. Legend has it that the ghostly drummer was actually one of the Lords Dacre who for unspecified reasons was living in concealment while pretending to be dead. However, he was a jealous man and the thought of other men courting his supposed widow made him so angry that he beat the drum as a deterrent and a warning.

A curious part of the drummer legend is the discovery and subsequent disappearance of an old iron chest. It was a cold winter's day in 1738 when two bored youngsters decided to explore the dark attics of the castle. Up the creaking stairs went the two friends, John Miller a young servant in the Hare family, and Will Lancaster, the son of the Steward. John carried the candle which only served to accentuate the flickering shadows on the wall. As they were going along the passage to the attics, Will lent forward and blew out the candle and they were submerged in darkness. Instinctively John put out his hand to the wall to steady himself and instead of a plain wall he found that his fingers were resting on a concealed recess. Excitedly the boys relit the candle and held it high to peer into the recess. They saw an old fashioned iron chest pushed against the far wall and they pulled it out and down into a room along the passage so that they could have a better look. The key turned quite easily in the lock and inside they found a jumble of papers, including some stiff vellum which Will said must be important documents. But they were not interested in them — what did fascinate the boys were two hammer-like objects of metal attached to the chest. What were they? If they were handles why were they so easy to detach? Will laughed and seizing them, he beat a tattoo on the lid of the trunk. At once they both became serious because the noise resembled the sound of a kettledrum being struck. John took the sticks and struck the chest too. There was no doubt about it — it was just like a drum. Perhaps they had found the phantom drummer! They rushed off to spread the exciting news. However, between the time they left and the time they managed to drag a reluctant Steward to see their discovery, the chest had mysteriously vanished. In 1892 the very same chest was rediscovered covered in rust in the underground passages of the castle by a Mr. Winchester, and it was placed in The Guardroom directly below the Drummer's Hall. But unfortunately nothing is known of its present whereabouts.

A grey lady also haunts the castle. The story begins with a later Thomas, Lord Dacre who lived well beyond his means and was obliged to sell Herstmonceux to pay off his debts. The estate was bought by George Naylor who had married Lady Grace Pelham, sister of the Duke of Newcastle and their only child, a daughter, was called Grace too. But the parents died young and by the age of five, little Grace was an orphan and the heiress to Herstmonceux. By all accounts she grew into a beautiful young woman who was looked after devotedly by her old nurse Margaret Beckett and her governess. The tragedy was that on the threshold of life with everything before her, Grace died suddenly in her twenty-first year.

What probably happened is that Grace suffered from what we would call today anorexia nervosa. Whatever the initial reason which triggered off the condition, it is agreed that young Grace died of starvation. A portrait has survived which shows Grace wearing a dress with a tight, narrow bodice above billowing skirts and it is easy to see how this sort of fashion could make a young girl obsessive about her weight.

Colonel Claude Lowther who bought Herstmonceux in 1911 encountered a young girl in the courtyard whom he took to be a gipsy girl out begging. But as soon as he spoke to her, she disappeared. He remembered especially that she was wringing her hands which were very white and shrivelled. This ghost was young Grace, known as the Grey Lady. Unlike the ghostly drum and the galloping Lord Dacre, the Grey Lady is silent and she glides about, thin and sad and insubstantial.

There is another beautiful and tragic lady who haunts Herstmonceux. Known as the White Lady she walks in the grounds, either near the moat or in the castle gardens. She is Georgiana Naylor, a late 18th century lady renowned for her brains as much as for her beauty.

An unorthodox lady, she went about clad in white from head to toe. Not only this but she was accustomed to riding in the park on a white ass followed, like Mary's proverbial lamb, by her tame white doe. Misfortune and ill-health came upon Georgiana. Some say it was because her doe was torn to pieces by a pack of stray dogs and that she never got over it. She went abroad to live and died at Lausanne in 1806. When the White Lady is seen in the grounds she is always wearing a long white cloak such as she used to wear. Sometimes she is seen riding her white ass with the white doe trotting along behind her.

7

The Girl with Golden Ringlets

TWO of the most evocative place names in Sussex are surely Amberley and the Wild Brooks. The Wild Brooks are in fact marshland liable to flooding at times from the river Arun. The church at Amberley is cheek by jowl with the castle which was once the favourite residence of the Bishops of Chichester. Naturally the church needed a vicarage to house a priest to minister to the people in the thatched cottages. It is this Vicarage which is haunted.

The Vicarage has cellars dating back to Elizabethan times but the house itself was completely rebuilt in the 1720s when Bell Carelton was the vicar. Even then it was only a one-storey building with a thatched roof and a verandah on the west side. It did not gain another storey until the late 1890s when the Rev. William Streatfeild was vicar. He and his family moved to Amberley in 1897 when his second daughter was two years old. Her name was Noel Streatfeild, later to become a prolific writer and one of whose best loved books is *Ballet Shoes*.

Noel often played alone at Amberley after her adored elder sister Ruth had to be sent away because the dampness of the place affected her delicate health. Noel had a younger brother and sister but they preferred each other's company. So Noel frequently amused herself in the garden. There was a mulberry tree and a hornbeam, but best of all, away from the house, there was an unusual rose tree which had flowers half white and half red and so was called a 'York and Lancaster'.

Noel adopted the rose tree as her own special possession but gradually she came to realize there was another little girl who also loved the rose tree. This little girl wore long white pantalettes and a crinoline. Her golden hair was parted in the middle and fell in ringlets on either side. Noel accepted her quite naturally and she did not feel any surprise at her presence although she only saw her in the garden. But the little girl was heard in the house quite often. She was inquisitive and liked to inspect new guests. When visitors came to stay at the vicarage, the handle would turn and the door of the spare room would open while footsteps pattered lightly over the floor. Visitors found this rather unnerving and one left hurriedly, even before breakfast!

There was a conspiracy of silence about the ghost because the servants knew and never mentioned it to the family while Noel never dreamed of telling her parents.

It is strange how the villagers also chose to remain silent about the ghost. It is possible they thought the vicar would be sceptical about such things or perhaps they feared he and his family would be frightened into leaving. Thus silence becomes a tradition.

In 1902 the Rev. W. Streatfeild left to become vicar of St. Peter's Church at St. Leonards and the new incumbent at Amberley was the Rev. Dr. G. F. Carr who arrived with his family. Mrs. Carr saw the little girl and she was so clear and lifelike that Mrs. Carr could not believe she was not a real child. She saw her through the dining-room window one afternoon and she watched her walk up the garden path towards the house. Mrs. Carr noted too the white dress and fair curls and she thought the child was about seven years old. Mrs. Carr waited for her to ring the front door bell and when nothing happened she went to ask the servants what had become of the child but they had seen nothing at all untoward.

There is a last satisfying footnote to this Amberley ghost. In 1904 the Carrs decided the vicarage must be renovated and an old wall was demolished so that the dining-room could be enlarged. While digging out the foundations, the workmen came upon a trench which contained earth of a different colour to the surrounding area. At about two feet below the surface which had once been covered by the old floorboards in the corner of the dining-room, the workmen discovered two skeletons, one of a woman and the other belonging to a child of about 7 years of age. It was remembered then how the Rev. George Arthur Clarkson, the vicar before the Streatfeilds and who had lived at Amberley for almost 50 years, had often complained about a bad smell in the dining-room. But nothing was ever done about it perhaps because it was put down to country drains.

The bones were buried in consecrated ground but not before several pieces had been carried off by the villagers as souvenirs. All the same the ghost of the little girl has not been seen again so it seems that she has found peace at last.

8

The Pale Lady of Pevensey

R ISING out of a flat countryside the rugged outline of Pevensey Castle is an impressive sight.

There are two candidates for the honour of being the pale lady who haunts Pevensey Castle. It is a coincidence that both ladies have a connection with Henry IV (one loosely, the other more intimately) but they both have fascinating stories.

In 1394 the Duke of Lancaster appointed Sir John Pelham constable of Pevensey Castle, which appointment he was to hold for life. When in 1399 this Duke's son decided to usurp the crown and make himself Henry IV it was a matter of honour that Sir John should support him against Richard II. So off he rushed with the Duke to land in Yorkshire and fight the king's army. That left his wife Lady Joan at home literally holding the fort.

It was fortunate she was not a wilting type of female for she suddenly found herself besieged by a large Yorkist army. She managed to smuggle a letter out of the castle to her husband in Yorkshire. In it she wrote in true restrained style 'if it like you to know my fare, I am here laid by in a manner of siege . . . that I may not out nor no victuals get me'. The letter had its effect and Lady Joan was able to hold on until the Duke's forces arrived to relieve the castle. But it must have been an anxious time for her as she paced the walls every day looking for a sign of her husband's return. What is more likely than it being her ghost whose misty shape is sometimes seen on the castle walls. It has been thought that the ghost was perhaps a romantic fiction. However, one August afternoon in the 1970s some youngsters did see a fragile looking female form standing on the walls which then vanished. A ghost was the last thing they expected to see while they were larking around on a summer's afternoon and they were so scared they ran off.

The other ghostly candidate is Queen Joanna of Navarre, a very interesting lady. In 1399 the very year in which Lady Joan was besieged at Pevensey, the Duchess Joanna of Bretagne first set eyes on Henry Bolingbroke soon to be Henry IV. What she saw pleased her mightily and never mind the fact that her husband was still alive (only just) and that she was the mother of nine children. But she had been married very young to an elderly husband and she was still a beautiful woman. Henry was widowed. When Joanna too became widowed later in 1399 she did what was expected of her and kept to her widow's weeds for two years but by 1401 she had engineered things to such a degree that she was soon married to Henry by proxy. Henry was devoted to her but alas the marriage did not last long because Henry died in 1413. At that time Joanna was on the best of terms with her stepson (Henry V) but six years later he had her clapped in prison.

The charge was a serious one — that of witchcraft. For a lesser mortal it would have meant instant death but Joanna was after all a Queen Dowager. She was also a woman of considerable wealth and it was most probably this fact which prompted the king's action. He was in need of funds and he had already tried to get his hands on Joanna's money; which move she had strongly resisted. What better excuse for seizing her possessions could there be than by accusing her of a serious crime and throwing her into prison without trial?

Joanna was arrested and ended up at Pevensey Castle under the charge of Sir John Pelham. She spent three long years there, deprived of friendly faces and made to wear ordinary clothes. But as Henry V lay on his death-bed his conscience began to trouble him about the way he had abused his step-mother. It was a burden which he did not wish to carry with him beyond the grave so he gave an order for her release and for all her possessions to be returned to her. Knowing what the loss of rich wearing apparel must have meant to her, he gave orders that she should have at once five or six costly new gowns to wear in such a style as she pleased.

The ghost of Queen Joanna is said to haunt Pevensey — her anxious prison for three years.

Opposite to the east gate of Pevensey Castle there is the timber-framed house known as the Mint House which was built in about 1343 probably on the site of the mint which produced coins in Norman times. The house was bought in 1542 by Andrew Boorde known as Merry Andrew who was also one of Henry VIII's physicians. The young King Edward VI once stayed with Andrew at the Mint House. Although he had studied at all the best medical centres in Europe, Andrew kept his sense of humour and thought nothing of selling his own preparations at local markets complete with humorous monologues on their virtues.

However there was no humour present at the Mint House in the 16th century when a grisly scene was enacted and it is thought the house has been haunted ever since. Many people have said they have seen a female ghost in the haunted chamber which is on the ground floor and is the smallest room in the house. Some years ago a man arranged to spend a night in this room to test the theory out. He took precautions against the possibility of practical jokes by locking the door and placing threads across the window. He lay down on the couch provided for him and as nothing seemed to be happening he soon fell asleep.

He was woken up by a curious tapping sound which seemed to come from the window. It was a metallic irregular sound and when he glanced at the window he was astonished to see a face pressed against the outside of the diamond-shaped window pane. He gave a startled cry and at once the ghost passed through the window and stood at the foot of the couch. She was dressed in the Elizabethan manner with a close fitting bodice, a very full long skirt, a small ruff around her neck and a head-dress of starched lace. After a few seconds she returned to the window but the man was so unnerved by her presence that he made for the door (which he found still locked) and went to summon his host and a friend. When they returned the ghost had gone and the threads across the window were still intact.

The popular explanation behind the haunting is that it was caused by a London merchant called Thomas Dight who had rented the Mint House. One evening in 1586 he returned home earlier than expected and found his mistress in the arms of a stranger. Dight was mad with jealousy and he caused the young girl to be bound securely and her tongue was cut out. Then she was forced to witness her lover being slowly roasted to death. His body was thrown into the sea and the girl was carried to one of the upper rooms and left to die. Apparently nobody knew about these crimes and they only came to light after Dight made a deathbed confession in 1601.

9

Mysterious Music

GEORGE Aitchison, Journalist and author of *Unknown Brighton*, was of the opinion that ghostly sounds are the last vestiges of a haunting. By inference it follows that soon there would be nothing left at all. However, it may be that mysterious music comes in a category of its own and is not dependent on other ghostly manifestations.

One of the best documented cases of supernatural music relates to the chanting monks of Poling. Martha Bates, who was born in 1870, had always been interested in ghosts. Perhaps it ran in the family because as a small child she had listened to her grandfather's stories of Sussex ghosts. Although these were told on dark evenings in the winter beside a flickering fire, she seems to have been enthralled rather than frightened. When she became a young lady with her hair swept up and wore the long sleeved and high necked dresses of the period, she began keeping a journal of her ghostly experiences.

She had heard about the monks at Poling and nothing would satisfy her except hearing the chanting for herself. She obtained permission from the owner of the house and she persuaded a relative to accompany her. Her companion was most carefully chosen because he was a professor of music and she judged that he would be able to identify any obscure music they might hear. He must have been a patient man or perhaps young Martha had infected him with some of her enthusiasm. At any rate they spent six long nights in fruitless vigil. On the last night they were sitting in a corridor in the oldest part of the house, huddled in blankets to try to keep warm, when they heard the chanting. It started off softly as though in the distance and then became louder as though a procession of monks were walking invisibly past them and the chanting faded away on the other side. The professor had no hesitation in stating that the music was a Gregorian funeral chant.

Confirmation of the phenomenon is provided by Philip M. Johnstone whose brother Sir Harry Hamilton Johnstone (1858–1927) owned the old farmhouse at Poling. Philip was an authority on Sussex churches and it was he who heard the chanting on several occasions when he went to stay with his brother. At first Philip was too surprised to register anything except the unexpectedness of the chanting. But as he became more familiar with the experience, he noticed that the chant was always the same. He was able to write down the notes he heard and he sent the score to a friend who knew about ancient music. The friend identified it as a Gregorian setting of the *Deus Misereatur* (the 67th Psalm) used at funerals. Philip Johnstone told the story to George Aitchison and to Arthur Beckett, author and editor of the *Sussex County Magazine* and they both had no doubts about accepting the truth of it.

The church of St. Andrew, Didling (south west of Midhurst) is small and stands by itself and is much praised for the antiquity and solidity of its pews. In the 1940s it became noted for something else — its ghostly choir. What is particularly interesting is that eyewitness accounts differ as to whether it was a single voice or a choir.

In the autumn of 1926 Z. A. Tickner went to visit friends who had recently moved house. He had never been to Didling before so he decided to explore. He walked around the farm and on being told where he could find the key, he decided to look inside the church. It was midday and the sun was shining. There was no sound from either farm machinery or traffic in the lane. Yet as he pushed open the door he distinctly heard the sound of men's voices singing plainsong. He looked again outside the church but nothing stirred and when he entered the church the singing had stopped. He searched inside the little church, even peeping behind the curtain but there was nobody there. He then went back and swung the door on its hinge but there was no sound of creaking. He never told anyone about his experience until years later.

On the other hand the late Rev. W. W. Whistler was certain that the ghost voice was a single very pure soprano. He was taking an afternoon service one Sunday and his congregation consisted of a handful of worshippers, all adult and some elderly. He was greatly astonished when he heard this pure voice singing in tune with the hymn and he knew that none of his flock could sing like that. He heard it two or three times singing a line or two of the hymn and then fading. The lady organist was delighted when he told her because she had heard the voice on several occasions and she had not liked to mention it before.

This story was printed in the *Sussex County Magazine* in 1943 and it soon prompted Z. A. Tickner to write in and tell about his experience there.

Unexplained music of a secular sort has been heard at Yapton. A recently retired man of 60 accompanied by his elderly parents had taken up temporary residence at Yapton while he searched for a suitable plot of ground on which to build a bungalow. One evening in the spring of 1956 two days after his arrival at Yapton, he was taking a stroll at about 9.30 p.m. It was a peaceful walk beside the old elms and high wall with here and there a cottage. He was surprised to hear the unmistakable sound of a lively polka being played on a quartet of stringed instruments. He felt sure a party was in progress and that when he rounded the corner he would see a big house alive with lights and the noise of people within. But all he found was an ordinary cottage with no brilliant lights. He stood there for about 10 minutes listening to the polka music, imagining that perhaps the party was being held at the back out of sight. It puzzled him that only the polka was played and no other sort of dance. He also found it strange that when he had moved several hundred yards from the cottage, he could still hear the polka as clearly as when he had been standing outside.

He went to bed just after midnight and he dreamed he heard the polka being played twice over on a single violin. Strange to relate, the following morning his parents said to him that he ought not to play his gramophone so late at night. They too had heard the polka played twice over. But the man did not own such a record and besides his record player was still packed up and there were no power points in the bedroom.

The only likely explanation is that music from a long ago party came through that night for some reason. The polka was a Bohemian dance which originated in about 1830. When it was introduced into this country it became a sensation. No doubt the older folk disapproved mightily and thought it the height of decadence while for younger people a party with polka after polka would have been very popular.

As a footnote to this chapter, there is a charming little tale from Cuckfield which relates that Martha, the ghost there, sometimes sings a folk song in the early hours. Perhaps she used to sing it years ago as a lullaby for a fretful baby.

10

The Lady in White

PRESTON Manor rests on ancient foundations because the place has been inhabited since Saxon times. Down in the basement there remains evidence of a 13th century stone built house. Over the years the manor has been rebuilt and extended and its present form dates from 1738. William Stanford bought the property and 980 acres for £17,600 in 1794. Thence the property devolved in 1853 on the heiress Ellen Stanford, then a five year old child. Lieutenant-Colonel J. Benett-Stanford was her only son.

For many years there had been a tradition that a ghost known as the Lady in White haunted the place. In the late 19th century the ghost had become such a regular visitor that she was expected to put in an appearance once every 4 to 6 weeks. Lieutenant-Colonel Benett-Stanford's grandmother Mrs. Macdonald who lived at the manor, seems to have struck a special chord of sympathy with the ghost and saw her many times. In fact her grandson went so far as to say the ghost was her great friend. (He never saw her himself, not being 'one of those people' he said). Other members of the family saw the ghost. Miss Di Macdonald saw her once when the house guests were having a tennis party. Di's shoes were hurting her so she ran into the house to change them. Half way up the main staircase she saw the ghost standing up on the landing. At first she did not realize it was the Lady in White and spoke to her but did not receive any reply. Then she put out her hand to take the lady's hand but her hand went through the figure and hit the wall. The ghost vanished.

Her sister Lily Macdonald saw the ghost in 1896. She was

standing in the drawing room adjusting a new lampshade when in walked the ghost and went right up to her as if she had something to say. Lily followed the ghost through the Billiard Room to the foot of the stairs but when she tried to put an arm around her to detain her a little longer, the ghost faded away.

The feeling in the family was that the Lady in White was trying to tell them something, so it was decided to hold a seance. The seance was held on November 11th 1896 in the Cleves Room, so called because the leather wall hangings are supposed to have belonged to Anne of Cleves. Around the table sat 5 people. They were Mrs. Macdonald and her daughter Lily, Mrs Goodrich Freer (a recognised medium) and her daughter. The only man present was Douglas Murray.

Even with the best of intentions an ouija board is not always a reliable instrument. So often it seems that malevolent spirits use the occasion for mischief. Instead of one straightforward ghost, the Preston seance attracted at least three. When the board was asked if the lady who haunted the place could make herself known, the answer was that there were two ghosts. Out of a welter of information it was established that the Lady in White was Sister Agnes who had died in 1535. But she was accompanied by another nun called Sister Caroline who apparently hated her. Unfortunately no reason for this antipathy was forthcoming other than the fact that Sister Agnes had been excommunicated by the church. When she died she had been buried in unconsecrated ground. But the reason for this drastic measure was not revealed. To add yet more confusion a Friar Martin appeared on the scene and said he had caused Sister Agnes to be excommunicated although no crime had been committed and the allegations against her were all lies.

Sister Agnes also disclosed that her body was buried on the terrace immediately outside what was then the dining room.

However, although Mrs Macdonald was sympathetic to the ghost's request she did not fancy having half her garden dug up on the off-chance of discovering some old bones. But the ouija board had started something and the matter was not going to be allowed to rest there.

Not long after the seance Mrs Macdonald's married daughter (Mrs. Magniac, formerly Di Macdonald) and son-in-law arrived at Preston Manor for a visit. There were other guests too and they all looked forward to a happy festive season. But one after another they began to suffer from severe sore throats. The symptom was regarded with great seriousness in Victorian times because had not the Prince Consort died prematurely of typhoid in 1861? The cause was said to have been the bad drains at Windsor so immediately Mrs Macdonald began to worry about the drains at Preston Manor. She summoned her surveyor and asked him for his opinion because after all she had spent quite a lot of money improving the drains not that many years ago. But the surveyor said the drains were in a bad state and needed urgent attention. So Mrs. Macdonald and her family removed themselves to a house in Brighton while workmen attended to the drains. She left the butler, Mr. Beesley, to keep an eye on things.

Part of the necessary work meant digging a trench near the house on the South Terrace. While engaged on this the workmen made an unexpected discovery on January 29th 1897 and Mr. Beesley was informed immediately. He in turn hurried into the manor. Ever the perfect butler, he did not wish to alarm Mrs. Macdonald so he telephoned her daughter Mrs. Magniac and asked her to come at once. What had been discovered was a skeleton and when the family physician, Dr. Blaber, arrived he pronounced it to be that of a woman and she had perfect teeth. The bones were an orange colour and Dr. Blaber thought they were at least 300 to 400 years old. However the position of the skeleton provoked a new mystery because it had not been laid in the ground in the normal fashion but rather it had been scrunched up into a hole, head to feet. If this was indeed the skeleton of Sister Agnes it raises the question as to whether she died of natural causes.

The bones were gathered together, placed in a box and the Preston gravedigger was instructed to bury it inside the churchyard. The bones were at last in consecrated ground. On January 29th 1898 Douglas Murray and Lily Macdonald held another seance in the Cleves Room. This appears to have been a less fraught occasion than the last seance. Sister Agnes came through undisturbed by other ghosts and said she was quite happy now that her bones had been reburied in the churchyard and she was content to rest peacefully.

By December 1898 Douglas Murray was able to write that it was almost two years since Sister Agnes had been laid to rest and she had not appeared since.

However the Lady in White did make one final appearance and it demonstrates the sympathy there must have been between her and Mrs. Macdonald. It was in November 1903 when Mrs. Macdonald had long been ill and confined to bed that Sister Agnes appeared at about 2 a.m. She stood at the foot of the bed staring intently at Mrs. Macdonald and Nurse Glasspool. It was as if she had come to say farewell. However, she must have been a real enough looking figure because the nurse mistook her for Lily Macdonald. Next morning Nurse Glasspool asked Lily somewhat plaintively if, next time she came in to see her mother at night, she would be kind enough to speak as it was rather unnerving to see her come and go without a word. Mrs. Macdonald died on November 28th 1903.

11

Unquiet Monks of Rye

RYE is an enchanting place and it would be surprising indeed if there were no ghost stories associated with the town. What is astonishing is that there are so many ghostly monks. It is as though the ancient streets still teem with monastic life. The monks belonged probably either to the Premonstratensian Canons or the Austin Canons both of whom had communities at Rye. The Austin Friars were established at Rye in 1363 and it is concerning one of their monks that the best known haunting is centered.

The monk was known as Brother Cantator because of his beautiful voice. No doubt he led his brother monks in their chanting. This monk happened to fall in love with a young girl of Rye called Amanda. So deep was their attachment that they resolved to leave Rye and perhaps start a new life together in France. But something or someone must have betrayed their plans because they had not gone far from the town before they were caught and taken back. Brother Cantator was walled up alive and for some days the monks could hear his fine mellow voice singing. Then shortly before he died he went mad and began to gobble like a turkey-cock. Young Amanda died of a broken heart.

Some say that his body was left where it was still walled up and that his ghost comes back to search for Amanda. Others maintain the young lovers were buried together and L. A. Vidler stated that the skeletons were uncovered still in each other's arms when the South Eastern Railway was being constructed in 1850.

His mad voice gobbling like a turkey-cock was heard in Rye up to the last century and for this reason they named a street Turkey Cock Lane. Andrew Green reports two sightings of Brother Cantator and interestingly enough one of them was in Turkey Cock Lane. It was in 1971 and milkman Graham Rhodes was delivering early one morning when he looked up and saw the robed figure of a monk at the end of the road. The other sighting was in 1952 at a hotel adjoining Dormy House where it is said the beautiful Amanda lived. Miss Marjorie Pellers was drinking a cup of tea sitting at the window when she saw a monk with a sad face standing near the party wall. Oddly enough both sightings report that the monk was wearing a brown habit whereas the Austin Friars are supposed to have worn black.

Perhaps also connected with Brother Cantator is a haunting at the Monastery Guest House, a building which contains some of the old monastic structure. The owners at the time of the haunting were Gerald Young and his wife. In 1958 the Youngs quite often heard the door bell ring at about 2 a.m. When Gerald Young went to open the door there was never anybody there. Except for two occasions, one in 1959 and the other in 1960 when he saw the foggy apparition of the head and shoulders of a monk but it was distinct enough to make out the roundness of his face.

At the corner of Watchbell Street and Church Square there used to be a pawnshop in the old timbered house. The manager began to notice strange scratching noises always on Friday evenings. The noises started in October and increased in volume each week. At last the manager decided that he and an assistant would stay late and see if they could find out what was causing the noise. The manager was convinced the shop was haunted. After they had waited a long time at the back of the premises from where the sound always emanated, they noticed a glow behind the barred window. Then they had a dreadful shock when they saw a monk with a frightful yellow face peering balefully through the bars. The manager rushed at the apparition with a stick but it soon vanished. The ghost appeared for several weeks and then it stopped suddenly. Some years later the house was bought by a woman who soon began to make some alterations. During the work some bones were discovered under the staircase and they were removed and buried in the churchyard. No sign of the monk with the awful yellow face has been seen since.

At another house in Watchbell Street there is another story of a monk with an unquiet grave. One day in the 1930s the cook from this house was enjoying her afternoon-off by sitting on the Look-Out terrace and admiring the view. All at once she became aware that she was not alone for sitting beside her was a monk in a brown habit. The cook was frightened by the apparition and fled to the safety of her kitchen. But when she got there she was horrified to find the same monk waiting for her. Unlike so many ghosts this one was quite articulate and he was able to tell her exactly what he wanted. Apparently he had been sent from Canterbury to bring some order and discipline to the dissolute monks but he had been killed for his pains and his body secretly buried in the garden of the house in Watchbell Street. He wanted his bones buried in sacred ground.

The cook lost no time in relating the whole episode to her employer. As her mistress was a Roman Catholic she in her turn hastened to tell the story to Father Bonaventure who was then priest-in-charge of St. Anthony of Padua. Father Bonaventure was evidently a practical man because as he said there was no indication as to where the bones lay and they might dig all over the garden and still miss them. His happy solution was to come and bless the whole garden and sanctify it. The action must have met with the monk's approval for he has not been seen again!

12

The Haunting of Brooker Hall

BROOKER Hall is a solid Victorian mansion at Hove designed in the Italianate style popularized by Osborne. It was built in 1877 for Major John Olliver Vallance (Lord of the Manor and one of the principal landowners in Hove) perhaps by way of celebrating his 30th birthday.

Brooker Hall was a happy family home until 1893 when Major Vallance died suddenly when he was only 46 and his children were still minors. Six years later his eldest son was killed in a carriage accident.

When the First World War broke out his wife Emma Vallance felt that Brooker Hall was too large for her now that the children had grown up and so she arranged for wounded soldiers to be nursed there.

After Emma Vallance died in 1924 Hove Council bought Brooker Hall for the bargain price of £4,000 and it has been a museum ever since 1926. The present caretaker affirms that although the atmosphere of the house is friendly there is often the feeling that one is not alone. But it is not a malevolent feeling — it is more like some concerned person hanging about to keep an eye on things. A previous caretaker reported that objects were sometimes moved around. Footsteps are heard quite frequently when the building is closed to the public and supposedly empty. Footsteps have been heard moving about upstairs but the footsteps heard most frequently occur downstairs. A door is heard to close and then there is the sound of footsteps walking down the corridor. The corridor in question is not part of the building to which the public has access but it is on the other side of the wall behind the souvenir counter in the entrance hall. According to the original plans this corridor led to the domestic quarters.

The room which used to be the breakfast room now serves as the curator's room. This room is always reported to feel cold although the heating is the same as for the rest of the house which has to be kept constant because of the furniture and other valuables in the museum. The caretaker's dog (not a little mite but a cross dòbermann/great dane) is not happy about the room at all and sometimes he will refuse point blank to enter the room and his hackles rise.

On January 4th 1985 some interested persons went to Brooker Hall together with a van full of ghost-hunting equipment including an ozone-sniffer. The idea was to see if the footsteps could be recorded but naturally the ghost chose not to walk that night. However, an interesting reading was taken in the curator's room when a certain area next to a large ecclesiastical embroidery registered two degrees warmer than the rest of the room. The embroidery is a vast affair set in a frame which stretches almost from floor to ceiling. It is a composite work made up of separate panels and strips in coloured silks and metal thread on linen mounted on velvet. It is dated from about 1550 and was donated to the museum in 1949. The figure of the crucified Christ is a prominent feature of the embroidery. Above the cross is a figure of God the Father while below the cross St. John supports the Virgin Mary. As soon as the ozone-sniffer was put in the vicinity of the cross it started to bleep and it did not matter from which direction the sweep was made (and it was made from all four quarters) the bleep began as soon as the cross was reached. It was here too that the temperature was two degrees higher than the rest of the room; not forgetting that the embroidery is enclosed within a heavy frame. Nothing registered with any of the other figures in the embroidery. There may be a prosaic explanation such as the type of wool used in the making of the body of Christ but it was a curious phenomenon to witness. The embroidery is not on display to the public at present but when it was, it is said that two girls who had been looking at it, left abruptly saying there were strange vibrations in the room.

There is also the tucking-in ghost. The caretaker has a young daughter who, when she was about ten years old, invited a friend of a similar age to stay with her. The friend was woken several times in the night by someone tucking her into bed. She assumed it was her friend's mother and asked her somewhat indignantly the next morning why she had kept on disturbing her.

To end on an odd note there is the story of a painter who was once working on his own at the back of the house on the north west side. He was painting away quite happily when he suddenly felt someone pinching his bottom. He looked round hurriedly but there was nobody in sight. The painter found this such an unnerving experience that he downed his paint-brush right away and rushed out. He refused to go back to Brooker Hall again.

13

The
Endless Search

HANGLETON Manor comes as a surprise because you do not expect to find a venerable house of Tudor origin in the midst of an area of modern housing. Yet there it stands today — a survivor from another age. Originally of course its setting was rural and remote and the house used to be sheltered by a group of ancient elms. Water for the household's needs was drawn from two deep wells while water for the horses and other livestock was available from an extensive pond close to the house. The house was rebuilt by Richard Bellingham (one time Sheriff of Sussex) between 1540 and 1553.

A haunted manor should be mysterious and an object found during restoration work done in 1927 was a secret writing desk. It was hidden in the thickness of the wall but there was nothing to distinguish the panel behind which the desk was hidden from the rest of the panelling. However, when the special panel was pulled down it formed a desk with drawers and shelves inside.

The Manor was sold to the Sackvilles in 1597 and the freehold remained in the family until 1967 although they did not live there personally. Continuity seemed to go with Hangleton Manor because for many years (some say 300) the place was tenanted by the Hardwick family who farmed the land. Family legend relates that the family (related to Bess of Hardwick) came from Derbyshire to help quell the smugglers

and ended up by becoming even greater smugglers themselves! Certainly the manor was well adapted to provide
hiding places for smuggled goods; there was a spacious chim-
ney at the back of the house which was rumoured to be one
such place.

Perhaps it was smuggling ghosts that the Hardwick
brothers used to hear often until they left the place in 1914.
The sound they used to hear was of heavily-booted men
trampling about the floors, talking and generally making a
noise. In the end the brothers just used to accept the ghostly
footsteps as one of the features of the house because they had
learned it was quite useless to try and see those ghosts in
person — they were never visible.

Another sound the Hardwicks grew used to came from the
Long Gallery at the top of the house. They were convinced
that it had been used as a skittle alley in Elizabethan days and
many was the time when they could hear quite distinctly the
noise of heavy wooden balls being rolled along the floor
followed by the sound of skittles being scattered.

One of the Hardwicks had a rare sighting of a male ghost.
He was sitting in a downstairs room when he heard the door
open and a figure clad in what appeared to be a white velvet
cloak came in. He was sure it was not a shadow or trick of the
light — besides it made a slight jingling sound as it walked as
though it were wearing spurs.

There are two female ghosts. One is rather shy and she is
more often sensed than seen. If she disapproves of someone
she will try to push that person gently out of the room. But it is
a subtle pressure. Others have felt her sweeping by leaving a
faint chill in the air; while some people have reported a
glimpse of the skirt of a brown silk dress brushing past.

The other female ghost is a much more tragic figure. No
date has ever been put on the tale for it has been handed down
by word of mouth. But it is genuine enough and recently a

stranger to the area had an experience of the ghost which seems to verify the outlines of the story.

It is a sad story of a young servant girl who came to work at the house and was seduced by her master. The horror when she discovered she was pregnant can well be imagined. When she gave birth she must have been by herself in her little attic bedroom because overcome with despair and exhaustion she suddenly snatched up the baby and hurled it to its death from the window. Some say she regretted her action immediately and desperately she tried to catch hold of the baby's clothes but it was too late. She screamed and screamed. Her ghost haunts the manor in an endless search for her baby. Sometimes shrieks in the night have been heard and knocks on the panelling but more often she is a harmless sad ghost.

The servant girl also manifests herself as a pair of white hands and it was in this guise that the Hardwick brothers knew her. The brothers used to sleep in a bedroom near the Long Gallery and they often saw two white hands on the door handle. There would be a knocking on the door and one brother would open it softly and see the hands holding the handle outside. Sometimes the hands would appear over the top of the door when it was ajar and then the door would be so difficult to shut that both brothers would have to put their shoulders to it.

Another witness of the white hands was R. Thurston Hopkins (1884–1958) the well-known writer, who had a particular interest in the place and wrote that Hangleton Manor had him compellingly under its spell. He knew the owner and he was allowed to come and go at will although the house was empty at the time. One night in November when it was stormy and bitterly cold, he walked over the Downs to the manor with his spaniel Duster at his side. All the blinds were pulled down in the house but this did not stop the ghost from displaying her famous white hands in a movement which

Hopkins described as fluttering. They appeared at a small window in the apex of the roof at the end gable of the house. At the same time as he saw the hands, his dog Duster behaved in a strange manner. He crouched low, his tail drooped down and he gave a series of shrill yelps, whereas his normal bark was deep.

Some years ago a young child was asleep in her bed at the manor when she woke up suddenly and saw a misty white lady standing at the bottom of the bed looking at her. She told her mother about the experience and her mother said that if it happened again she was to say to the lady 'I am not the child you are seeking'. When the lady did appear again the child remembered the words and spoke them to the ghost who quietly faded away. The story comes right up to date with the manor once more providing a roof for small children. These two were sleeping peacefully at either end of a long upstairs room and their father had just stepped in to make sure all was well when he became aware of a faint shape leaning over the youngest child.

Recently, two local people and a relative visiting from Wales went to Hangleton Manor for a quiet drink (it is now a public house). The Welshman knew nothing about the manor's history but on stepping over the threshold of the room which is thought to have once been the chapel, he staggered slightly. His friends asked anxiously if he was all right and he had to sit down before telling them what was the matter. He said he had had the most vivid mental picture of a baby in long night clothes falling and he could hear loud and terrible shrieks; there was also the sense of water everywhere. This raises the question as to whether the baby fell into water or whether the unfortunate girl drowned herself.

14

Some Eastbourne Spectres

IN 1918 when she was ten years old Pamela Frankau (later the well-known novelist) was attending a school called Claremont at Eastbourne. It was there that she saw a ghost in broad daylight. An unusual feature of the sighting was that she saw the ghost first of all reflected in a mirror. As she came up the stairs, Pamela could see the cupboard standing on the landing. The cupboard was ajar and the mirror on the front of it reflected a view of her bedroom whose door was wide open. In this glass she noticed something moving across the bedroom floor. She was puzzled because the other two girls with whom she shared the room, she had just left in the garden. As she was wondering who it could be, the ghost ran out of the room and it was like a dwarf because it was a humped white shape. The ghost scuttled to the middle of the landing where it faded away. Although it sounds indistinct, she was quite sure it was solid but she did not tell anyone about it until she was grown up.

Another haunted school is Eastbourne College. This one is not so odd as Pamela's but it is infinitely more pathetic. It is the ghost of a young boy who found everything too much for him and he hanged himself in one of the dormitories. His pale shape has been seen standing still near a bedroom doorway as though he were waiting to ask something. There is also an icy cold feeling in one part of the corridors.

As a contrast to this youthful ghost, the next ghost belongs to an old man who had become too attached to the armchair he used to occupy at a nursing home in Gorringe Road. The old man must have spent many hours sitting in that comfortable armchair mulling over the events of his past life and when he died it did not seem to make much difference to him. The other residents could sense his presence and hear his laboured breathing in the sitting room every evening.

A man living in a cottage in Watts Lane had a nasty experience one night when he woke to find a ghost clutching his legs and immobilising him in his bed. A gentle haunting is one thing but a strong-armed ghost is quite another! Not surprisingly the man sought the help of a Roman Catholic priest the very next day. The priest came and sprinkled holy water around the house. This seemed to settle the ghost who had also been accustomed to turning on the bathwater and opening doors unexpectedly. The ghost was the cottage's late owner who had apparently taken an active dislike to the new owner's wife. When she was away, all was peace and quiet but when she was in the house the ghost became active. After the priest's visit she was away from home for about 5 years but as soon as she returned the ghost was troublesome. He was seen walking up the stairs and he was no misty shape either, because every detail of his face and clothes could be seen so there was no mistaking his identity. Also the couple's children heard a voice calling from the attic on several mornings. The house was eventually sold.

An 'outside' ghost as it were has been seen near a roundabout where Willingdon Road and King's Drive converge. She is dressed in grey and is seen in late afternoon. Her sudden appearance can cause havoc to motorists who think she is a real person and they feel convinced they have hit her because there is no time to brake. One motorist has seen her twice with a year's interval between the sightings. Her clothes have been described as a costume in the style of the 1920s and people have linked her with a woman golfer who was killed here in the 1920s in a bad smash which killed other people too.

15

Shadows aboard the Hygea

THE boat was called the *Hygea* after Hygeia the Greek goddess of health, daughter of Aesculapius god of healing. It was not a fanciful name chosen because the owner was fond of Greek mythology but a practical name because the vessel was the Port of London Health Authority's barge. She was moored at Gravesend from the 1930s until the 1970s and she served as the headquarters for the medical officer. For ships coming in to London with sickness or injury amongst their crew, sending the afflicted man to the *Hygea* in the jolly boat was the quickest way to get medical attention. The cases the MO had to deal with ranged from toothache to tropical diseases and from smallpox to broken limbs. It is probable that in all those years some people must have died aboard the Hygea. Mr. Doug Dear was Harbourmaster for the Port of London for 20 years and he knew the vessel well but he never heard any tales of the boat being haunted. As seamen are traditionally supposed to be superstitious it is fair to assume that if anything unusual had occurred aboard the *Hygea*, word would have got around.

After her long service (and she was built originally as an ammunition barge in 1917) the *Hygea* was retired. The story now moves to the quiet waters of Littlehampton marina where the *Hygea* now rests albeit with a different function and another name. She was bought by Mr. Alan Becker and renamed the *Seahorse*. In July 1984 she opened for business as a floating restaurant and pub. It should have been a peaceful retirement for the old boat but in the event something restless was aboard.

The first reported happening was experienced by Mr. Chris Schwar, the nightwatchman. He was by himself on board and it was a hot muggy night. In the early hours he became aware of a cold draught and thinking that some window might have been left open, he went upstairs to check. But all was secure so he returned to his room. The chill persisted and Mr. Schwar was so cold that he was obliged to put on his fur coat to keep warm. Associated with the chill was a feeling of terror and his hair did literally stand on end. He could think of no other way of combating his fear other than barricading himself in by wedging a chair against the bulkhead. The cold and the terror lasted for an hour and a half and then the temperature returned to normal.

The haunting did not confine itself to one part of the boat and the bar and kitchen were also affected. On another occasion Mr. Schwar happened to see the hanging pot plants inside the main bar area start to swing vigorously although the *Seahorse* herself was quite static.

Perhaps Mr. Schwar's strangest experience was the one which also occurred late at night. He was sitting in front of the fire in the bar area when he suddenly saw human shadows on the wall in front of him. He knew there was nothing behind him except the quiet waters of Littlehampton marina, yet the life-like shadows continued for fifteen minutes. By this time he had come to accept that there was something mysterious about the *Seahorse* and nothing ever had scared him so much in his life as his first experience.

Miss Mandy Milson, waitress, was also sitting in the bar late at night with friends when they heard the door at the top of the stairs opening and closing. As there were several of them there, they had no hesitation in searching the boat but of course there was nobody about.

Mr. Danny Lazarus, the chef, maintains there is a cold spot in the kitchen by the sinks. It is particularly noticeable when it occurs on hot days. He saw once a person of short stature standing at the bottom of the stairs leading to the lower deck restaurant. When he crossed the room to check, there was nobody there. Working in the kitchen he often gets the feeling that someone is watching him. On one occasion he came aboard with some tarot cards shut in a box which was wrapped in his apron. As he got to the stairway the tarot cards shot down the stairs and he never did find one of the cards again.

All these occurrences were reported in 1984. Mr. Becker reported in 1986 that ghostly activities aboard the *Seahorse* had quietened down. It seems that whoever or whatever it was must be learning to accept the situation. The vessel had been repainted red and white in the intervening time. Was it a happy inspiration or did Mr. Becker know that red and white are the traditional medical colours, as witness the barber's pole dating from the time when barbers were surgeons too? Also it was the practice for warships (like the Victory) to paint red the floor of the cockpit where the injured were brought so the blood would not be so noticeable. So perhaps the ghost felt more at home in a ship of these colours and thus settled down.

The Curse on the Priory

MICHELHAM Priory was built to take advantage of a natural bend in the river Cuckmere and when the great moat was dug out, the Priory became an island. However, this did not happen overnight; although the Priory was founded in 1229 the moat was not made until the late 14th century.

There have been many changes over the years and the most dramatic occurred in 1536 when the Priory was closed on the orders of Henry VIII. Thereafter the church was razed to the ground but some of the old buildings survived and were incorporated into two Tudor houses. Michelham was a monastery of Austin Canons and as they were all priests, the Dissolution did not hit them as hard as other religious houses because they were able to earn their living as parish priests.

A ghost dressed in the robes of an Austin prior has been seen at the Gatehouse. He was friendly and anxious that visitors should go to the Priory towards which he seemed to point an invitation. Perhaps this was John Leem, Michelham's most outstanding prior who held the office for almost 40 years. There can be nobody with a better right to linger at the Gatehouse than the man who was responsible for its construction in about 1395.

A female ghost wearing a grey dress has been seen on the bridge in front of the Gateway. Reports about her differ, some say she stands on her own looking into the moat with a sad expression. It is said that she was a member of the Sackville family whose daughter fell into the moat and drowned. This seems unlikely because although Michelham Priory belonged to the Sackvilles for almost 300 years, they did not live there as they had extensive property elsewhere and they preferred to rent Michelham to tenants. The Child family were tenants for 70 years. Perhaps the Grey Lady is Mrs. Child still mourning for her 5 year-old son Robert who was playing in the nearby watermill when his clothing became entangled by the wheel of the machine used for dressing the flour and he was strangled. Other reports state that the Grey Lady has been seen leading a small dog towards the Gatehouse. But all agree that the lady is thin and ill-looking.

Arthur Beckett, writing in 1911, thought the Grey Lady walked at night but he did not specify which room she visited. People sleeping in that particular room could expect the lady dressed in grey silk to walk up to the bed, draw aside the curtain and gaze at the occupant. She would stay there looking for a minute or two and then as though disappointed at what she found, she would move softly away, her silk dress rustling.

Another female ghost has been seen in the large Tudor room on the ground floor, once part of the farmhouse. Nobody seems to have noted the style or colour of her gown except that it was Tudor and she was also a ghost in a hurry. Perhaps the object of her haste is a man in a black cloak who was once seen descending in majestic ease a now-vanished staircase. Just after he made his exit, the bemused witnesses saw the ghostly lady running after him.

One of the most interesting exhibits at Michelham Priory is the Bellarmine jar which was excavated in 1972. It is currently on display in Tudor Room II. Also inside the glass case are some rusty pins and an unidentified dark lump which were found inside the jar. It is fascinating to speculate whether the jar was used to lay a curse or lift a curse. A jar of pins was a well known remedy against evil but the inclusion of something which might be an animal heart would seem to signify that a curse was being laid. The Bellarmine Jar raises more questions than can ever be answered but it is an indication of strong feelings about the Priory and adds to the air of mystery.

17

The Musician's Farewell

HUBERT Parry, although a prolific composer, had an enormous zest for outdoor life. As well as walking, he loved to play tennis and was often to be seen regally pedalling a bicycle along the Sussex lanes. He loved the sea and the rougher the weather the more he enjoyed standing on the pier at Littlehampton, watching the waves boil and hiss around him. On calmer days he enjoyed building sandcastles on the beach with his young friends and he was as happy as they were paddling about and exploring because another of his interests was to examine marine specimens under his microscope.

The Parrys had first come to Sussex in 1876 on the recommendation of a friend because Mrs. Parry's health was causing anxiety. The Parrys decided to make their home here and they built their own house at Rustington. Parry chose Norman Shaw as the architect because he admired the design of his gentlemen's houses which were based on Sussex Wealden examples but with a Victorian dash. Norman Shaw was probably used to his clients knowing exactly what they wanted but he could not have encountered a more enthusiastic man than Parry, who was involved with everything to do with his new home. Parry's daughter laid the foundation stone of the house at 'dear Rusty' (as Parry was fond of calling Rustington) and a veritable army of 46 men worked on the site. If the number seems excessive it must be remembered that the Victorians loved their details and so skilled craftsmen in different materials were necessary. Parry busied himself in the grounds, doing much of the planting out himself. On July 22nd 1881 Parry and his family moved into their new residence which they had christened Knight's Croft and they were well pleased. They did not forget their workforce and a special feast was laid on for them. It was a typical gesture from a man who was by all accounts genial and sympathetic and in later years when his walrus-style moustache had turned white, he resembled everyone's favourite uncle.

The first winter they spent in their new home was very cold and there were snow drifts of up to 9 feet. Parry took advantage of the cold snap and went skating on the pond at Rustington. On wet days he would spend hours practising Bach's Preludes and Fugues. When he was not composing he was busy writing articles on music because he was a learned musician as well. But his most popular anthem is of course *Jerusalem* which has been adopted by the Women's Institute as their hymn. It could be termed a Sussex hymn because William Blake is supposed to have written the words while he was living at Felpham. When Parry had completed *Jerusalem* he handed the manuscript to Sir Walter Davies with a modest 'Here's a tune for you'.

For 37 years Parry enjoyed living at Knight's Croft and it is fitting that in his closing years he actually was a knight. He died at his home on October 7th 1918. His body was cremated and his ashes were placed in the crypt of St. Paul's Cathedral. But is it any wonder that Sir Hubert found it hard to leave his beloved house at 'dear Rusty' straight away?

The new owner of Knight's Croft was startled to see his ghost walk straight through the wall. But she said she was not in the least upset by it because he looked his usual jovial self and nobody could be frightened by such a kind old man. Sir Hubert's ghost took one last lingering look around his old home as if to reassure himself that all was well and then he vanished.

18

Something Nasty at the Rectory

BEATRICE Molyneux had some rather odd manifestations to contend with, which she wrote about in 1937. Twineham Rectory was the home of Beatrice and her father when he was rector of the small village of Twineham near Cuckfield. The Rectory was comfortable enough and it was set in large grounds but the sheltered life in the house was punctuated by odd happenings like the sound of hurried footsteps running up the stairs and stopping halfway, or the bedclothes being tugged away or a sudden cold draught on the forehead. Some experiences were pleasant like the appearance of a smiling lady clad all in white. She had long dark hair which fell below her waist and she carried a basket of red roses. She opened the door and came in and stood inside the room, smiling and reciting the verse

> 'A flasket, a flasket
> A four-and-twenty basket.'

After which she withdrew, still smiling, and closed the door behind her. This ghost only appeared twice, once to Beatrice and once to one of her sisters. As it was on separate occasions the sisters were able to compare notes and they found that they agreed completely about the details of dress and figure.

However Beatrice was the only witness to a nastier haunting which happened when she was quite young. She seems to have taken the experience in her stride without being in the least afraid. At the time she was playing on the landing — a favourite place because it was long and dark and full of doors. She was playing with a rubber ball. She had discovered that when it hit the ceiling little bits of whitewash fell off and it amused her to collect the white flakes up in her handkerchief. All at once she saw a movement at the end of the landing and to her astonishment she saw a glove crawling along the floor towards her. It was a large black kid glove and the fingers were rounded out as though there was a hand inside. She stood still and watched fascinated as the glove crawled slowly onwards! Then it vanished and she found herself gazing at nothing.

Another unpleasant phenomenon was witnessed by Beatrice, her two sisters and the maid. Beatrice and her sisters Mary and Edith shared the big night nursery. The view from the window over the countryside was beautiful and this was some compensation for the frightful bilious wallpaper with which the room was decorated. Mary and Beatrice shared a large four poster bed (but without the posts) and one night Mary woke Beatrice up to tell her there was a rat scratching under the mattress. Beatrice sat up and she could hear the awful scratching clearly so she pulled the bell-rope hard and summoned the maid. Meanwhile all the commotion had disturbed the other sister Edith. They all heard the scratching and they were convinced it was a large rat. The maid was the most frightened of them all so Beatrice seized the bed coverings and pulled them onto the floor leaving only the under sheet on top of the mattress. The centre of the mattress began to rise so Beatrice grabbed hold of her pillow and whacked the lump again and again. The action goaded whatever it was to fury and the scratching and tearing increased while the mattress was lifted up to about a foot in height. When the scratching suddenly stopped they gazed in horror at a flat, still, mattress. The maid and the girls stood on chairs for safety while Beatrice turned the whole mattress right over but there was nothing to be seen. The clawing sounds continued for about 6 months but it gradually became weaker until it stopped altogether. The girls apparently got so used to the sound that they never let it interfere with their sleep again!

19

The Restless Spirits of Battle

IT is the one date which everyone knows — 1066, the Battle of Hastings. To stand on the Lower Terrace at Battle Abbey and look down over the green fields, it is hard to visualize the long drawn-out battle between 14,000 combatants which took place here. This is especially true in early summer when trees and grass are a fresh green and the buttercups wave in the breeze. Nevertheless there is a tradition that the ground still weeps blood. It is not as preposterous as it sounds because there is iron in the soil and after a heavy downpour streaks of red can appear.

The Anglo-Saxon army under King Harold was drawn up on the ridge by the grey apple tree as the old chroniclers tell us while William the Conqueror's army occupied lower ground. The battle started at 9 a.m. on October 14th and continued until dusk. The English were in a strong position and remained solid despite repeated charges from William's forces. The latter feigned a retreat which did lure some of the English down from their height in hot pursuit, but the rest remained immovable until the light began to fade.

King Harold's two brothers Gyrth and Leofwine had already been killed in the fighting but the final blow did not fall until William ordered his archers to fire high. A chance arrow struck Harold in the eye. The earliest source for the arrow story is the Bayeux tapestry and some historians maintain he was not killed by an arrow at all but was cut down by

Norman swords. What seems most probable is that Harold was disabled by the arrow and before anything could be done, some Norman knights broke through his house-carls and killed him. The next day two priests from Waltham Abbey searched the battlefield for Harold's body but they had to report they were unable to find it. Then Harold's mistress Edith went in search of her lover's body and found it. She had his body buried at a secret place near Hastings.

Some say that the ghost of King Harold lingers on at Battle, traversing the ridge or standing motionless gazing down the valley as he did on that October morning watching the Normans forming up. Some say that he has even been seen re-enacting the dreadful moment when he was struck by the arrow but the anti-arrow faction tend to dismiss this out of hand.

It would be interesting to know whether William the Conqueror ever heard stories about Harold's ghost. At any rate he ordered an abbey to be built on the battlefield in about 1070 with the high altar sited over the spot where Harold was killed. Today the spot is marked with a simple stone slab which is almost invisible under the shadow of the nearby tree.

In 1972 near the Chapter House a young boy noticed a man holding a long sword and asked his father about him. But nobody else could see the man. If it was the ghost of a Norman knight, he might have been one of the leaders as a sword was a sign of prestige as well as a weapon. From examples which have survived it can be estimated that the blade of a Norman sword would probably have measured 90 centimetres in length.

As might be expected the ghost of a monk has been seen. He was spotted one evening gliding along the pavement towards the Gateway of the Abbey. Perhaps he was one of the final monks who with their abbot were given their marching orders during the Dissolution of the Monasteries. It was on May 27th 1538 that the abbot surrendered Battle Abbey and the estate went to Sir Anthony Browne, Henry VIII's Master of Horse. The abbey was pulled down straight away but parts of the monastic buildings were left including the Abbot's House, the Gateway and the outer wall.

There are two other ghosts connected with the Abbot's House. One is a lady in red whose footsteps and rustling dress have been heard on the stairs while a lady in grey has been seen going along the corridor leading to the Abbot's House. The latter must have had some impediment when she was alive because her footsteps sound painful, as though she were limping. One could imagine an aged housekeeper going on her nightly rounds to check that everything is in order, though she might be a member of the Browne family who continued to own Battle Abbey until 1715. Or she might belong to the Webster family who owned it subsequently.

Augustus Hare tells of another ghost, but perhaps she has ceased to haunt as nobody else makes a mention of her. His story concerns Lady Webster who came to stay at Battle Abbey not long after her marriage. One night she was settled comfortably in her four poster bed when someone drew back the curtains. Looking up she saw an old woman of terrifying appearance gazing at her. The old woman continued her inspection for a few moments before she turned and left the room. She was so solid looking that Lady Webster concluded she must be some aged family retainer. Seconds after the apparition had left, her husband entered the room and she asked him at once who that dreadful old woman was. He had seen nobody and if she had been a person of flesh and blood he would have seen her in the passage outside. So Lady Webster revised her opinion and felt sure she had seen a ghost. Even in old age she could clearly remember the details of the old woman's dress.

20

Haunted Churches

CECILE Woodford in her book *Portrait of Sussex* recounts the experience her father had as a young man. Sometimes he went to the evening service at All Saints, Patcham. One cold Christmas Eve the congregation was sparse and the young man could not help noticing a lady sitting in a nearby pew. She was dressed in grey and she was tall and thin. But what struck him most forcibly was the extreme paleness of her face. He began to wonder uneasily if she might be ill which would not be surprising given the severity of the weather and the thinness of her clothing. So he leaned across the pew and draped his overcoat around her shoulders. His coat was a heavy melton and ought to keep anyone warm. Several times during the service he looked at her to make sure she was all right. As the congregation stood to sing the last hymn he glanced across and was amazed to see that she had vanished. His coat lay crumpled on the seat of the pew. But nobody had left the church or he would have noticed as he was sitting next to the door. When he told the story at the village inn he was informed that he had seen the Grey Lady of Patcham. Whoever she was, she conferred a lasting benefit on his overcoat which refused to wear out and was still as good as new 70 years later.

A priestly ghost has been recorded in St. Nicholas's Church, Arundel. It was not seen by human eyes but was photographed inadvertently. It was one day in 1940 when a highly respectable solicitor from Arundel stepped inside the church. His hobby was church architecture and he wanted to take some interior photographs while the church was empty.

When the print of the altar was developed it showed the unmistakable outline of a priest in Mass vestments standing at one side. The solicitor was very surprised because when he pressed the shutter he was not aware of anything unusual and he was quite sure the church was deserted.

There are ghosts connected with the old church of St. Peter, Preston. Some members of the choir said they had seen a ghost which emerged from the south side of the church and disappeared in the churchyard. They were not the only eye-witnesses because one Sunday evening two people were walking past the church when they saw two ladies in mediaeval costume walking in front of them. They watched the ladies as they approached the stile, the ghosts then turned right and disappeared through a terracotta tombstone on the west side.

In the churchyard of St. Thomas, Winchelsea, there is a tradition of a black ghost in a red uniform although there is no clue as to his identity. Negroes were not unknown in this country and many were brought in as slaves until the slave trade was abolished in 1807. It was fashionable in the 18th century to have a black slave and many important families owned one. Perhaps the Winchelsea ghost belongs to this category. Alternatively he could have served as a soldier.

A ghost has also been seen in the churchyard of St. Mary, Westham not far from Pevensey Castle. But this is a modern ghost who wears an ordinary grey suit. Sometimes he is seen leaving the church while at other times he is seen walking towards it. Mr. Michael Stone is a recent eye-witness who saw the man in grey in September 1978. He states that he had been to see Pevensey Castle several times and on this occasion he decided to visit the church also. When he reached the gateway he had a clear view of the man whom he judged to be 5 feet 10 inches in height. Mr. Stone smiled and said 'Good afternoon' but as he started to open the gate, the man vanished. He realised afterwards that the man must have looked perfectly ordinary or else he would not have greeted him. However it was a bit of a shock when he disappeared so suddenly!

21

Wicked
Dame Ann

IN 1691 Charles Sergison purchased Cuckfield Park, an elegant Elizabethan mansion and the Sergisons continued to own the place until this century. But it should not be thought the continuing surname meant an unbroken male succession — far from it. It became an established custom for future husbands of Sergison heiresses to assume that surname on their marriage. This may have encouraged a line of strong-minded females and the most formidable of the lot was Mrs. Ann Pritchard Sergison known in many stories as wicked Dame Sergison. This lady was heiress to Cuckfield Park but she was not recognised as such until she was 57 years old.

She had a strong character but the same could not be said of her brother Colonel Francis Sergison. While he was in an Irish debtor's prison he married a fellow inmate who rashly promised him an heir. After his release Colonel Sergison was away for a while and when news of his imminent return reached his wife, she panicked because she was not pregnant as promised. The best she could do was to buy for 7/6d a four-day old baby girl from a servant girl. The transaction took place in a Dublin pub. The Colonel was delighted with his new family. In due course they returned to England and lived at Cuckfield Park. When he died in 1812 at the age of 45 his wife and 'daughter' continued to live in the house where the young girl was brought up with every comfort consistent with her station in life.

The truth came out after a long drawn out enquiry instituted by her aunt, Dame Ann, who became the rightful heiress in 1820. All those years of bitterness erupted in a rash of settling old scores against one and all. She lived until she was 85 and she died unlamented. In fact the locals said she was too wicked to rest in her grave and her ghost was sighted performing a most unlikely feat for an 85 year old — swinging on the oak gates at the entrance to Cuckfield Park. Perhaps she could not bear to leave the scene of her bitter triumph. But horses shied on nearing the gates and carters were afraid of going along that stretch of road.

There are two versions as to how her haunting was made to cease. One version states that the grandson had the wit to replace the old oak gates with new spiked ones made of iron and iron is commonly thought to be a good protection against evil. The other story goes that three clergymen met at midnight in Cuckfield church and carried out a service of exorcism. This seems unlikely becaue an exorcism is usually carried out on the site of a haunting. But to preclude any doubts on this score the gossips added darkly that the clergymen caused the ghost to be drowned in the font.

Cuckfield Park itself, with its twisting chimneys and mullioned windows, has a ghost of its own. The Sergisons had grown so used to it that it was like one of the family and they never gave it a second thought. But to visitors who were unaccustomed to being on familiar terms with ghosts, a chance meeting could be quite unsettling. In 1890 a young cousin of the Sergisons called Frances Blencowe was invited to a family wedding. She met the family ghost on the stairs and mistook her for a real person. At the time Frances was going up stairs and as she was in a strange house with many people, it was no surprise to see an unknown lady coming down the stairs. She stood aside politely to allow the lady to pass and the lady swept past smiling graciously at her. Frances fully expected to be introduced formally to the lady later on but when she mentioned it to her hostess, she was met with a laugh and an explanation that she must have met the ghost.

The ghost is still there today. The Jaques family who sold Cuckfield Park and its 40 acres of land in April 1987 called her the Grey Lady and said she went back some 300 years. During the 9 years the Jaques occupied the house they never saw the ghost in person but they have been aware of her presence from time to time. She makes the hair stand on end. Nobody has an explanation as to why the Grey Lady walks the house.

22

Sweet Scents and Ghastly Vapours

O F all the senses, smell is most closely associated with memory. A particular scent can carry us back to childhood quicker than anything else. As smell registers in our earliest consciousness so it seems that in some cases a certain scent is the last thing to fade away.

Smelling a ghostly smell is quite a different experience from seeing a ghost which might possibly be explained away as a trick of the light, a vivid imagination or a waking dream. But having the nostrils assailed by a smell which should not be there cannot easily be dismissed.

It is interesting to note that a pleasant scent was often associated with the passing of saints. At the moment of death a sweet smell was released into the room which could be sensed by all those attending the deathbed. It was known as the odour of sanctity and it was held to be one of the factors proving that the departed was indeed a saint.

So pleasant smells are nothing to be scared about. Mr. Peter Thorogood bought the beautiful timber-framed house at Bramber known as St. Mary's for £165,000 in 1985. Much time and expense have gone into the restoration of the house in preparation for its opening to the public once again. Mr. Thorogood reported in April 1987 that a strong scent of roses pervades the place from time to time. The scent does not confine itself to a particular room either but has been detected in various parts of the building which dates back to the 15th century.

The well-known actor Norman Wisdom never smelled the ghostly smell at his home, Laker's Farm, Pulborough. But his mother certainly did. When he was interviewed in September 1975 he told the story of how his mother had been in bed one night when she had suddenly noticed a strong scent of apple blossom. She said the scent pervaded the whole room but she had no idea that it might be supernatural. Later she felt very hot and pushed back the bedclothes. Then she felt as though someone were leaning over her and gently blowing in her face. It was not a frightening experience because the presence seemed quite benign and even laughed softly. It turned out that she had experienced the same manifestations which had been witnessed down the years by other people. Like St. Mary's, Laker's Farm is also a venerable building and dates back to the late 15th century. Norman Wisdom sold the farmhouse in 1980 and moved to the Isle of Man.

Not far from Pulborough is West Chiltington which boasts a charming story of a more down to earth smell — the aroma of frying bacon. The story behind the haunting is that in the early days of one particular house's history, a resident monk was much addicted to the taste of bacon. So powerful was his passion that he could not resist frying himself a little piece even on fast days when meat was strictly forbidden.

Two 'flower' hauntings now; one pleasant and the other sad. Mr. Holdstock, former organist of St. Mary's, Northiam, records that once when he was playing the organ he became aware of the scent of arum lilies although there were no such flowers in the church.

In an old curio shop in Meeting House Lane, Brighton, the lovely scent of fresh flowers often made itself apparent in the 1950s. They were no ordinary flowers either but delicate hot house blooms like orchids. The reason behind the haunting is that a young man often used to bring flowers home to his mother who owned the curio shop from the flower shop where he worked which was called Fountain Court. The flower shop owner was a wealthy man and he was obviously fond of the youth. However, when the young man announced his engagement to a Brighton girl the relationship deteriorated, there were violent quarrels and eventually the shop owner strangled the youth in a jealous rage. Several people have seen the unfortunate young man and all agree that he had abundant fair hair and wore a sports jacket. He was also reluctant to leave the curio shop much to the annoyance of the next owner for the ghost would often hide a piece of china or sit in his favourite chair.

The ghost hunter Andrew Green lives at Robertsbridge. His home was originally two farm cottages built in 1725 but Mr. Green believes they were constructed on the site of a much earlier building. The ghostly smell which he and many guests have witnessed is the pungent aroma of tobacco emanating near one of the inglenook fireplaces. It always occurs at the same time — 5.30 p.m. One can just imagine a former inhabitant settling down to smoke his evening pipe after a hard day's work. It is amusing to recall that a down to earth LBC Radio reporter came to interview Mr. Green in 1974 and right in the middle of the proceedings the reporter became aware of an overpowering smell of tobacco although he could see for himself that nobody in the room was smoking. The reporter found it an unnerving experience.

A complete contrast to these innocuous scents is the smell of sulphur which has always been regarded as linked with evil, in fact one of the Devil's trademarks. In the 1970s the ghost hunter Dave Stringer of Lancing was with a group of friends in the churchyard of St. Nicolas, Brighton when one of them sensed a strong smell of sulphur. More alarming still were the experiences of two families at a house in Truleigh Close, Woodingdean, Brighton. In 1977 Mrs. Dubeau was unsettled to find that her council house was visited on occasions by a cloud of sulphur. It made her 14-month old daughter Joanne sob with fear and the couple had to move the baby into their own bedroom to soothe her. Mrs. Dubeau felt that something dreadful must have happened in the house and that the evil lingered on. The Dubeau family were not the only ones affected by the smell of sulphur and a previous tenant Isobel Roper and her daughter Vicky confirmed the story. In fact she had invited a priest to bless the house and for a time the sulphurous smell ceased.

23

Spirits
of the Trees

AT South Heighton, a hamlet on the Downs overlooking the
Ouse near Newhaven, there was a line of ilex trees
(evergreen oaks) which ran through the churchyard down the
hill and through the front garden of the lovely old farmhouse.
They must have been a magnificent sight but the new tenant
who took over in the early years of this century was unim-
pressed. He said the trees made his rooms too dark and he
decided to cut them down. Before he did so he was warned by
the villagers that felling the trees would bring a curse on the
house but he took no notice. When the trees had been chopped
down he was pleased because his house was now light and
airy. However, it was also filled with strange whisperings and
sighings. The tenant might have been happy but his family
could not stand it and eventually they moved away. Nobody
could be induced to live in the house, not even a young couple
from Newhaven who were offered it rent free for a year. People
avoided the house at night because a white face with large
dark eyes could be seen in the window over the front door
peering mournfully into the night.

At length the local vicar decided the situation could not be
allowed to continue so he came and exorcised the rooms.
Thereafter the hauntings ceased. But was this due to the
exorcism? George Aitchison preferred another theory because
when he passed by the place in the 1930s he noticed there
were vigorous shoots sprouting out of the old ilex stumps.

By a strange coincidence another story connected with trees comes from Denton, which was the next village south from South Heighton. In the autumn of 1933 Mr. and Mrs. Sydney King, their 12 year old daughter and Mrs. Heaseman, Mrs. King's mother moved into the Manor House at Denton. Above the front door a stone was inscribed with the date 1724. There were 14 rooms and a mysterious cellar with a bricked-up doorway, said to be the entrance to a secret passage leading under the adjacent graveyard to the church.

All was peaceful until one Saturday when Sydney King decided to cut down some trees on the front lawn. They had been planted by a former occupant of the house who, as local people remembered, had declared that they should never be felled. The very next day Mrs. King saw an apparition. She was walking along one of the passages when she saw a ghostly figure. It was so unexpected and frightening that she screamed loudly. The noise brought her husband rushing to her aid armed with a stick. He beat at the apparition with the stick but it passed straight through and hitting the wall behind, it broke. The ghost was only seen once and the worst part of the haunting were the loud knocks which started to occur regularly. They followed a pattern, being always 4 blows at a time and coming either at 20 minutes to the hour or 20 minutes past with an interval of 5 or 6 hours.

The knocking was heard by all the family, plus two visitors and the rector of Denton, the Rev. E. Pinnix and his wife and a reporter from the *Evening Argus*. The rector said a prayer, hoping that the earthbound spirit might be released but it did not seem to do much good and the knocking continued unabated. The cellar door also began to behave oddly and it was often found wide open when it had been securely bolted shut earlier.

The constant knocks began to get on the nerves of the King family and poor Mrs. Heaseman who was in her seventies had been heard to utter horrifying shrieks. They decided to pack up and leave the house altogether. After they had gone a policeman and several men kept a watch outside the empty Manor House. At about 10.20 p.m. a loud knocking was heard to reverberate from the house — four knocks the same as usual. The men at once unlocked the front door and searched the house from top to bottom but nothing was found.

24

Martha of the Dell

THE chapel could be said to be the heart of Brede Place because according to Father John the chapel stands on the site of an ancient sanctuary where 2,000 years ago a shepherd dwelt. The shepherd was a holy man and people flocked to consult him. Father John is the ghost priest who haunts the chapel. He is not like other ghosts in that he is earthbound because of crime or violent death. He remains at Brede because he chooses to do so to help less fortunate souls on their way. He has work to do and he will not leave until it is finished. His influence is wholly beneficial. If anybody is disturbed by other less benign spirits at Brede, there is always sanctuary in the chapel and in the old priest's room because no evil force dares to intrude there. In the 1890s the chapel was used as a place to store apples amongst other things but the chapel was restored to its original use by Clare Sheridan's grandfather Frewen. During the work a human skeleton was found buried beneath the altar steps and later Father John was to tell Mrs. Sheridan's psychic friend Shirley that he had been buried in the chapel.

An unpleasant haunting is the ghost of Ralph Oxenbridge whose family were responsible for many alterations to Brede Place in Tudor times. The psychic woman called Shirley had a most unsettling experience when she tried to contact the Oxenbridge ghost as he tried to entice her into leaving her body saying that it would be far easier to converse when she had left her shell. The spell was broken by making the sign of the cross. But not before Shirley had had an insight into his violent death. She saw Ralph Oxenbridge fast asleep. He was wearing a red coat and his sword and high boots were on the floor. She saw a man in black creep into the room carrying a sword and she watched in horror as he plunged it into the chest of the sleeping man. It is known that the Oxenbridges had a long standing feud with their neighbours the Cheneys over a boundary dispute. The Oxenbridge reaction to this outrage was to burn down the Cheney house and kill the murderer.

Perhaps spirits find it easier to manifest themselves at Brede than in other places. In 1952 Mr. Roger Frewen, Clare Sheridan's nephew, bought back Brede Place after it had been out of the family's care for five years. (The Frewens bought the house originally in 1712). He felt strongly that his ancestors approved of his action and especially his grandmother. Before her marriage she had been one of the celebrated Miss Jeromes of New York and her sister had married Lord Randolph Churchill. One evening at Christmas time in 1954 Roger Frewen went into a small room adjoining the main bedroom which was once used to store all his grandmother's bits and pieces. He became aware of the unmistakable scent of violet perfume such as his grandmother always used.

Lady Randolph Churchill visited her sister at Brede Place and she was put in the haunted bedroom but she did not enjoy the experience and she refused to visit Brede again. However, Winston Churchill occupied the same room on another occasion and slept undisturbed. The ghost is that of a lady who died suddenly and tragically in that room about 200 years ago although nobody seems to know the exact circumstances. In May 1953 a 15-year old Harrow schoolboy saw the ghost at 2 a.m. and she was wearing a dress with high shoulders and a long full skirt.

Part of the grounds is also haunted. Clare Sheridan used to

be aware of it on the hill at the back of the house, in the dell and at the upper gate. Sometimes at dusk she would feel as though someone were trying to push her away from the woods. Clare Sheridan seems to have been unusually sensitive to the spirits of Brede but being an artist and a sculptor as well as coming of a long line of Frewens must have given her a special affinity to the place. Anyway she was determined to find out who was haunting the dell. The story as related to Mrs. Sheridan and her friend Shirley is rather tragic. The ghost is of a young girl called Martha who was raised at Brede from childhood and became a servant at the big house. She lived during the reign of Henry VIII. Martha thinks of herself as very wicked because she allowed the two sons of the house to use her body and she also stole all sorts of things. Her one good memory is of her great love for the woodman and their times together in the dell. It was on his account that she stole her lady's jewels. There was a tremendous uproar in the house when the loss was discovered but meanwhile the woodman had escaped with the jewels leaving poor Martha to take the blame by herself. At this time she was pregnant — not by the woodman but by one of the two sons. Whether the lady of the house knew anything of this or whether the loss of her precious jewels was excuse enough, we do not know. But she paid some men to drag Martha up the hill where she was hanged on a tree overlooking the dell. Afterwards they burned her body with the garden rubbish. Martha believed she was wicked and totally unlovable but she liked to stay in the dell where she and her lover had once been happy. She was also deeply concerned about the trees and she wanted to make sure nobody would chop them down. The ghost was pathetically pleased that the two women should show her such friendship and compassion.

25

The Berwick Gardener

THIS tale is set in the village of Berwick in the days before it became famous for the wall paintings by Vanessa and Quentin Bell and Duncan Grant.

If a visitor chanced to come to Berwick asking for Henry Duty, the villagers had no hesitation in replying 'You can't miss his cottage, it's the one with the garden'. Now that might seem a silly thing to say because all the cottages in this village close to the South Downs had a bit of garden. What they meant was that Henry's was different. Whereas the villagers looked after their gardens after a fashion and sometimes only tidied them up after prolonged nagging from their wives, Henry tended every inch of his garden with loving care. Winter and summer, morning, noon and evening, Henry was to be seen busy at his gardening. It was as if he were mounting a constant vigil against attack and it was true that no other garden in the neighbourhood flourished as did Henry's.

In the front garden he grew old fashioned cottage flowers in such a profusion of colours and scents that the bees ambled about on heavy wings, laden with pollen. Although everyone in the village agreed that the flowers were a fine sight, Henry's real passion was reserved for the vegetables he grew in the back garden. He was generous too and many a poor household blessed Henry's name for providing some good vegetables to add to their thin soup.

The king of vegetables as far as Henry was concerned was

the potato. Not everyone agreed with him and even at that time there was a lingering prejudice amongst the old folk who considered the potato a new fangled crop. But not though in Henry's hearing because he could get very heated indeed in defence of the potato. Of course he did not let them know that one of his little secrets was always to plant his seed potatoes on Lady Day.

Henry was a village institution and if any child had a query about plants or insects off they would trot to ask Henry's advice. Then one day in 1855 the garden was empty and there was no sign of Henry. The villagers knew at once that something must be wrong because only the day before he had mentioned it was time to get his seed potatoes planted out. So they went to his cottage and pushed open the back door. Or at least they tried to push it open because Henry lay on the stone floor behind it, dead. He was wearing his gardening boots but one boot-lace was still undone. 'Poor old Henry' they said, shaking their heads sadly, 'it don't seem right to call a gardener to his rest with the spring planting coming up'.

The cottage did not remain empty for long and soon another bachelor moved in by the name of William White. He too enjoyed gardening which the villagers said was a good thing for they felt that poor Henry would never rest easy in his grave if his precious garden were to be neglected.

One day as William was washing his hands at the kitchen sink, he was startled to see the ghost of Henry Duty standing before him. The shock left him speechless at first but gradually out of the depths of his memory, he dredged up the correct formula to use on such an occasion. 'In the name of the Father, of the Son and of the Holy Ghost, what troublest thou, Mr Duty?' Henry's ghost replied solemnly that he had buried some seed potatoes in a corner of the garden and he indicated where they were to be found, then he vanished.

William lost no time in digging up the seed potatoes and planting them out properly as directed. He did the work to the best of his ability for he had the notion that old Henry was keeping an eye on him. But he never saw the ghost again and neither did any of the villagers. It appears that once he had delivered his message, and satisfied himself that his precious vegetables were in safe hands, Henry was content to lay down his gardening tools at last.

Bibliography

Ghosts
Braddock (J) Haunted Houses (1956)
Brown (RL) A Casebook of Military Mystery (1974)
Coxe (ADH) Haunted Britain (1973)
Finucane (RC) Appearances of the Dead (1982)
Forman (J) The Haunted South (1978)
Green (A) Ghosts of the South East (1976)
Green (A) Our Haunted Kingdom (1973)
Green (A) Phantom Ladies (1977)
Haining (P) Ghosts (1974)
Hallam (J) Ghosts' Who's Who (1977)
Hole (C) Haunted England (1940)
Ludlum (H) The Mummy of Birchen Bower (1985)
Mackenzie (A) A Gallery of Ghosts (1972)
Maple (E) Supernatural England (1977)
Moore (R) Sussex Ghosts (1976)
Squires (P) The Ghost in the Mirror (1972)
Underwood (P) This Haunted Isle (1984)

Sussex
Beckett (A) The Wonderful Weald (1911)
Brighton Gazette and Herald 22:12:78 17:9:82 16:6:84
Deacon (JL) Ancient Rye (1911)
Evening Argus 19:9:75 3:12:76 31:12:76 6:2:79 18:8:82 3:9:83 31:5:85 31:10:85 1:11:85 8:11:85 23:12:85 19:9:86 9:4:87 21:4:87
Hare (A) The Story of My Life (1896) Vol 1
Hare (A) Sussex (1861)
Scales (WF) The Story of Hangleton Manor (ND)
Staines (Revd EN) Dear Amberley (1977)
Sussex Archaeological Collections Vols 13, 25
Sussex County Magazine Vols 4, 5, 11, 13, 14, 17, 22, 27
Sussex History Vol 1
Sussex Life 1974 1976 1980
Vidler (LA) A New History of Rye (1934)
West Sussex Gazette 19:9:80 11:10:84 18:10:84

General
Bull (A) Noel Streatfeild (1984)
Longhurst (H) My Life and Soft Times (1971)
Sheridan (C) My Crowded Sanctuary (1945)

Index

INDEX